FURNITURE 2000

modern classics and new designs in production

Schiffer Publishing Ltd

4880 Lower Valley Rd. Atglen, PA 19310 USA

Leslie Piña

ISBN: 0-7643-0496-8
Printed in Hong Kong

Designed by Leslie Piña
Layout by Bonnie M. Hensley
Typeset in Zurich BT

Library of Congress Cataloging-in Publication Data

Piña, Leslie A., 1947-
  Furniture 2000 : modern classics a new designs in production /
Leslie Piña.
    p. cm.
  Includes bibliographical references and indexes.
  ISBN 0-7643-0496-8 (hardcover)
  1. Furniture design--History--20th century--Catalogs. I. Titles.
NK2395.P57   1998
749.2'049'075--dc21   98-11507
                                                         CIP

Published by Schiffer Publishing Ltd.
4880 Lower Valley Road
Atglen, PA 19310
Phone: (610) 593-1777;
Fax: (610) 593-2002
E-mail: Schifferbk@aol.com

In Europe, Schiffer books are distributed by
Bushwood Books
6 Marksbury Avenue
Kew Gardens
Surrey TW9 4JF England

Please write for a free catalog.
This book may be purchased from the publisher.
Please include $3.95 for shipping. Please try your book-
store first.
We are interested in hearing from authors
with book ideas on related subjects.

dedicated to the designers and makers of great
modern furniture classics -- past, present, and future

Acknowledgments

I would like to extend my thanks to all of the individuals representing the companies included in this volume for providing photographs and information. A partial list includes Behshad Shokouhi at Arc Age; Véronique Slechten at Artifort; Amy Chouinard at Baker; Bob Halper at Specsource for Breuton; Nancy Reedy at Cassina; Margot Walker at Design America; Judy Burns for Girsberger; Frederick Poisson at Halcon; Chuck Hartlage at Haworth; Bob Viol and Rich Rutledge at Herman Miller; Millie Adams and Kurt Hanson at ICF; the Marketing Department at KI; Messeret Sertse at Knoll; Joan D. Revere at Kron; Laura Thompson at Luminaire; Dr. A. Bianchi Albrici at Memphis; Hans Bulterijst at Palazzetti; Carolyn A. Smith at Shaker Workshops; Heather Itzla at Smith & Hawken; Teresa Will at Steelcase; Melissa Desota at Steelcase Design Partnership; Yvonne Reitemeier at Tecta; Mitsumasa Sugasawa at Tendo; Martha Wadsworth at Thonet; Elaine Caldwell and Momo Krauß at Vitra; and Peg Cambio at Zero.

Thanks again to Paula Ockner for proofreading and to Douglas Congdon-Martin, Peter Schiffer, and the others at Schiffer Publishing.

Contents

Introduction

There have been many discussions and definitions of modern, some more intelligible than others. From convoluted art historical discourse to the promotional jargon of manufacturing companies, certain aspects of the concept have been mutually agreeable. Most dictionary entries define modern as "pertaining to present or recent time; characteristic of contemporary styles (in the arts), with emphasis on individual experimentation and sensibility." This straightforward definition applies to furniture and should be agreeable to all.

Modern furniture is non-traditional, non-historical, or even anti-historical. Except for post-modern statements with subtle and, hopefully, witty historic references, there has been a conscious effort by its designers to avoid history. Yet, in the past this was not an issue. Historically, furniture styles have all been modern in their day. What would now be called "period furniture" was once new and in fashion. Chippendale or Louis XV designs from the mid-eighteenth century looked absolutely modern to those who commissioned and crafted them. The same furniture today is called period or antique. By the second quarter of the nineteenth century, the history of furniture, as it had been, ended. The new Victorian furniture was different because of the mechanization of woodworking and other craft industries with subsequent affordability and universal availability, a widespread use of historic styles with a lack of understanding or concern for accuracy, and an endemic craving for surface decoration, such as carving, gilding, and inlay, as well as for bizarre upholstery.

Mechanization was crucial to a nineteenth-century modernizing society but, ironically, it was used in the arts to make antique reproductions and novelties. With few exceptions, like Thonet's use of bentwood and Shaker efficiency, opportunities to produce modern furniture were ignored and lost. Historic revivalism and interior clutter reached claustrophobic proportions. By the early twentieth century, a new group of forces could be identified. First, the new professional interior decorator popularized different versions of historic revivals. These were more "academically" correct, more true to the period from which they were borrowed. Manufacturers turned out quality copies for the well-to-do and cheaper copies of copies for the populace. Not unlike the case of their Victorian predecessors, stylistic integrity often became lost in the commercial frenzy, and cheap generic non-styles called "borax" mesmerized the average consumer.

At the same time, modern art and architecture were being quietly born. Leading pioneer modern architects -- Wright, Mackintosh, and especially those affiliated with the Bauhaus -- also explored furniture design. Although many pre-war experiments with modern designs and materials could have been, and should have been, mass-produced, they were not. Instead, they were designed and made for specific installations from tearooms to individual residences. Other than their originality and high cost, the early modern pieces often had little in common with each other. Some used traditional materials (wood), while others experimented with tubular steel; crafting techniques varied; quality ranged from good to bad; and attention to function and comfort was as varied their styles.

The Second World War affected the manufacture of everything, including furniture. Pre-war fascism had already frozen creativity in parts of Europe, but the closing of the Bauhaus in 1933 was more like putting a rock in a gopher hole -- the creature simply dug its way out and reappeared, this time, in the United States. There was a European (especially German) brain drain, notably in science and the arts, and modernism in the United States was infused with this wave of talent from abroad. Raw materials and industry had been tied up during the war in both Europe and the United States, but 1945 marked the beginning of a new era. With newly developed materials and mass production methods, the furniture industry was given an unprecedented opportunity to modernize.

The industrial design profession was still an international youngster, born in the United States in the late 1920s and raised in the 1930s with pioneers like Gilbert Rohde. The field was maturing when George Nelson, followed by Charles and Ray Eames, appeared at Herman Miller's doorstep in Zeeland, Michigan right after the war and Rohde's (unrelated) death. Although parallel events were taking place in European centers from Scandinavia to Italy as well as in the United States at Knoll, Nelson and Eames have been credited with starting the first large-scale modernization of the American furniture industry.

Nelson was a master of simplicity in his visual and verbal statements. He could communicate the essence of form through elegant industrial design and eloquent prose. Naturally, Nelson wrote about the subjects that he designed, especially furniture. In the late 1940s he observed that there were already misconceptions about what modern furniture was and what it was expected to be. He was one of the first to point out that presumed attributes, such as function were highly overrated. It was assumed that because modern furniture had been relieved of its superficial ornamentation, the remaining form had magically-enhanced function. The cliche "form follows function" had led to some odd assertions about the nature of modern design, including furniture.

Smooth surfaces were presumably functional if the objective was mass production, but surfaces had little to do with, for example, the act of sitting. An uncomfortable carved chair will be equally uncomfortable without the carving. Some of the classic modern designs of the early twentieth century are far less functional than many historic pieces. The eighteenth-century Windsor chair is very functional, as are many other historic designs. Yet Mackintosh, Wright, and Reitveld are not remembered for their attention to human comfort -- nor are the unique and equally compelling late twentieth-century designs by Memphis. Yet all of these names made significant contributions to modernism.

Another misconception Nelson pointed out was the expectation that modern furniture is mass produced and therefore affordable. Unfortunately, simplicity of design is not necessarily simpler to produce. In fact, without moldings to mask poor joinery, construction techniques must be more precise. And precision is costly. So all modern furniture is not necessarily more functional (unless it is specialized and driven by ergonomics), and it is not necessarily economical or even mass produced. By definition it is new and not dependent on tradition or past style. It does include individual experimentation, but it is not arbitrary or without direction. Rather than performing the work of a decorator or a craftsman, the designer sets out to solve a problem, while at the same time striving for a visually pleasing product. It can be the need for efficient storage or for a comfortable sitting position. The design must be manufactured and offered at a relatively affordable price. Most of all, it must have eye appeal. In other words, the designer of furniture must be an artist who is knowledgeable about things like ergonomics, materials, technology, and marketing.

The perception of designers, manufacturers, dealers, and other people who talk about furniture is that there are two disparate categories -- contract and residential. Contract furniture is for the workplace and public places away from home; residential furniture, as the name denotes, is for the home. In other words, one is for places where people work, and the other is for places where people live. In the United States (more than in Europe) there is little crossover. To keep this segregation clear, even the styles differ. For the most part, twentieth-century residential furniture has been, and still is, based on historic styles. Even at the threshold of the millennium, it is no more surprising to see a room filled with uninspired wannabe eighteenth-century look-alikes as it is to see state-of-the-art electronics perched on them. Americans have an uncanny capacity for accepting visual and cultural anomalies.

Modernism has found wider acceptance in the area of contract furniture than residential. What is curious is the division between work place and living place. Don't people in fact live where they work and also work where they live? Most workers spend about one third of their day, maybe a fourth of their lives, in the workplace. The majority of the other three fourths is probably spent at home (including sleep time). Between the two, we live most of our lives with furniture. We eat on it, write on it, place things on it, work at it, and store things in it and on it. We decorate with it, put our feet up on it, lose things in crevices, and watch the cat jump onto it. We sit, lounge, play, make love, sleep, give birth, and die on it. Furniture is as much a part of our lives as any material object can be. Yet we casually allow others to design, build, and even select it for us without batting an eye. Many people give little thought to, or have little say in, the posture of their backs or the pleasure of their spirits. They are more particular about details when ordering a meal than of a chair that will support a species-specific weak back and give comfort to a hyper-sedentary bottom for years, perhaps decades.

So why not have well-designed, functional, comfortable, durable, and good-looking furniture in both the workplace and the residence? And if it happens to have modern styling consistent with a modern life style, why not use it at home as well? These are questions that the people at companies represented in the following pages have been asking. Although the modern classics and other new designs have been perceived primarily as contract furniture, they have also been attracting the attention of a growing cult of modernism collectors and dealers, plus interior designers, architects, and a general audience that is noticing the lack of style and choice in the residential marketplace. The great designs are classics because they are still great by any standards. Equally good new designs will become the classics of the future. Softening the barrier between contract and residential furniture is apt to become one outcome of a more widespread acceptance and appreciation of modern design.

In 1952 William J. Hennessey wrote in *Modern Furnishings for the Home*:

> This is a catalog of a style -- compiled with the sincere conviction that a definite need exists today for a single, comprehensive reference guide where the individual and personal schools of Modern design may be compared and properly evaluated.
>
> The output of contemporary home furnishings during the past few years has been staggering. Much that we see is excellent, of sound design, intent and craftsmanship. Much, however, depending on surface values and showmanship in its bid for attention, seems destined, like all sham, for early obsolescence. Intelligent selection by both professional and layman becomes increasingly more difficult.

This statement is still applicable, and this book, nearly half a century later, is intended to be one reference of modern furniture design and an aid to intelligent selection. The pictures in the following pages depict the good and the extraordinary designs that are currently in production and available primarily to the trade. Only some designs are known, and fewer are available, to the general public. Although there is a growing number of sophisticated consumers interested in their personal environment and interior design, there is a definite lack of accessible information about outstanding contemporary furniture. There is even less known about many of the early classics of modern design.

With few exceptions, the modern classics are from the twentieth century. In some instances, more than one company is producing a design, because it is in the public domain (no longer under patent protection) or is simply being copied. Where a design has been produced continuously by a company, or where one company produced it earlier, I have tried to show it by that company, even though others may also be offering it. It is sometimes difficult to determine which company's product to represent, and I apologize for any errors.

In order to present each item as accurately as possible, all photographs and descriptions have been provided by the producers or providers, i.e., distributors. Any omission of information -- designer, date, dimension -- is because it was not included in company literature. Dimensions are given either as overall or, for example, seat depth rather than overall depth. This should be apparent by comparison with other items. Any omission of specific companies, designs, or designers does not imply that they are less important or less interesting than those shown. There are many excellent smaller companies and even some major furniture manufacturers that have not been represented in this volume. Some may have been inadvertently overlooked; others did not reply to my request to borrow photographs. There simply had to be a place to end. Office furniture alone can fill a volume, and only a small, but representative sample has been included here. Lighting is a whole subject unto itself. In a field as dynamic as furniture design and manufacture, future revisions of both products and publications are expected. Since pricing is the most frequently revised aspect, I have not included it, but the list of sources can lead to pricing information by request.

The book is divided into chapters according to function -- chairs are for sitting, while lounges, sofas, and beds are/can be for reclining; chairs that swivel and roll are intended primarily for office use; things are placed *on* tables and *in* case pieces. Chapter organization is strictly visual, so items are grouped by design attributes -- size, shape, proportion, color -- and where it makes sense, by materials -- wood, metal, plastic, glass, stone, upholstery, and their combinations. Since this is a source book of currently produced furniture rather than an historical survey, pieces are not necessarily in chronological order. However, because of design similarities, some groups of furniture -- bentwood or tubular steel chairs, for example -- may appear to be grouped by era. The dates of recent designs are not always given, so most of the undated designs probably are of relatively recent date. Most early modern classics are easily identified by their visual attributes, and in most cases they are also dated. Even to those already familiar with these designs, the earlier dates can be surprising -- which is probably why they are classics.

My goal is to whet the reader's appetite with some of the classic modern furniture that has been made continuously, reintroduced, or reproduced, along with a sample of more recent proto-classics and other new designs. I also hope to make these designs better known and more accessible to both the trade and the public. Rather than promote any particular company or designer, my aim is to support all good modern design. If these pictures succeed at heightening awareness and enjoyment, they will have also served that end.

Please note:
Dimensions are in inches
- H = overall height from floor to top, unless specified, such as seat height
- W = usually overall width from outside to outside
- D = usually overall depth from front to back, unless specified, such as seat depth
- L = overall length
- DM = diameter

1: Chairs

Thonet
No. 14 Chair
Designed by Michael Thonet, c. 1855.
Simplicity, durability, and affordability
made this design the most popular
commercial chair of the nineteenth century,
and it was later referred to as the first
consumer chair. In the 1870s an estimated
1,200 of this model were sold daily, and by
1920 about 30,000,000 had been produced.
Steambent beechwood frame, shown with
upholstered seat, available with original
cane.
H 32", W 16", D 22"
Courtesy Thonet

Thonet
Classic Vienna Café Chair, No. 18
Designed by Michael Thonet's sons, c.
1876.
The most important and best selling
model produced after the death of
Michael Thonet; steambent beechwood
frame, natural cane seat.
H 34-1/2", W 17-1/4", D 21"
Courtesy Thonet

Thonet
No. 4 Café Daum Chair
Designed by Michael Thonet, c. 1850.
The selection of this design for the
fashionable Café Daum coffeehouse
marks the rapid acceptance of Michael
Thonet's designs for the emerging
affluent consumer society in the mid-
nineteenth century. Later, this chair was
altered for mass production and was
known as the No. 4 chair. Steambent
beechwood frame, natural cane seat.
H 34-1/2", W 18", D 21"
Courtesy Thonet

Thonet
Adolf Loos Chair
Designed by Adolf Loos, c. 1899.
A new era of bentwood furniture began
when Thonet manufactured this model by
architect Adolf Loos for his renovation of
the Café Museum in Vienna. Though
similar to the No. 14 model, it is more
complex and visually interesting.
Steambent beechwood frame, wood
veneer seat.
H 33-1/2", W 22", D 17"
Courtesy Thonet

Thonet
Classic Hoffmann Chairs
Designed by Josef Hoffmann, c. 1933.
Hoffmann version of twentieth-century
bentwood with emphasis on geometric
form; steambent beechwood frames,
upholstered foam cushion seat or natural
splined cane seat and back.
H 31-1/2", W 17-1/2" or 20-1/2", D 20"
Courtesy Thonet

Thonet
Frank Chair
Designed by Josef Frank, c. 1929.
Often attributed to Josef Hoffmann, this
design is a departure from Frank's work in
more exotic materials; original in bright
colors and popular during the Depression;
steambent beechwood frame, upholstered
foam padded seat.
H 32", W 17-3/4", D 19-1/4"
Courtesy Thonet

Thonet
Viennese Nouveau Chair
Designed by Josef Hoffmann, c. 1908.
Geometric decorative elements on back
splat, steambent beechwood frame;
adaptation with upholstered foam
padded seat.
H 36", W 18", D 21"
Courtesy Thonet

Thonet
Edel Chair
Designed by Studio Diemme Architectural
Design, c. 1990.
Inspired by Austrian Modern design;
beechwood steambent frame, wood splat
back, optional upholstery.
H 34-3/4", W 17-1/2", D 19-1/2"
Courtesy Thonet

Palazzetti
Stacking Chair
Design attributed to Robert Mallet-Steven, 1930.
Steel tube and sheet metal structure; seat of sheet metal or pear wood, available with fabric upholstery.
H 32-3/8", W 17-3/4", D 20-3/8"
Courtesy Palazzetti

Thonet
Regina Side Chair
Designed by Thonet design staff, c. 1985.
Epitome of Thonet design; solid beechwood frame, upholstered foam padded seat/back, plywood seat interior.
H 36", W 19", D 21-1/4"
Courtesy Thonet

Thonet
Hoffmann Side Chair
Designed by Josef Hoffmann, c. 1902.
Steambent beechwood frame; upholstered foam padded seat, back, and outer back; adaptation of original Hoffmann design in 1902 J & J Kohn catalogue.
H 36-1/2", W18", D 21-3/4"
Courtesy Thonet

Thonet
Deco Café Chair
Designed by Marcel Kammerer, c. 1910.
The details of the arc back and arc motif supports subtly induce the sleek deco style; hardwood frame, upholstered seat.
H 33-1/2"; W 22", D 17"
Courtesy Thonet

Thonet
Viennese Café Chair
Designed by Josef Hoffmann, c. 1911.
Hardwood frame with geometric motif in
back splat, typical of Viennese Modern
design; upholstered foam padded seat.
H 39", W 18", D 21-1/2"
Courtesy Thonet

Thonet
Fledermaus Chair
Designed by Josef Hoffmann, c. 1907.
Designed for the Fledermaus Cabaret, a
theater-bar where members of the Wiener
Werkstätte socialized. Steam bent
beechwood frame, upholstered seat with
recessed welt over sinuous steel springs,
elastic fabric straps, rubberized fiber pad
and foam. The spherical element was
integral to Secessionist design language
and also provided structural support.
H 29-1/2", W 22-1/2", D 18"
Courtesy Thonet

Thonet
Gropius Chair
Designed by Michael Thonet's sons, c.
1880.
Early bentwood model used for an
adaptation by Walter Gropius in 1952;
steambent beechwood frame, wood back
and saddle seat.
H 29-1/2", W 22-1/4", D 21"
Courtesy Thonet

Thonet
Gropius Captain's Chair
Designed by Walter Gropius, c. 1952.
Thonet first introduced designs by Ameri-
can architects and independent designers in
1952. This Thonet adaptation is of oak
veneer molded plywood frame, with solid
oak scooped saddle seat.
H 31", W 22", D19"
Courtesy Thonet

Thonet
Anniversary Chair
Designed by Joe Adkinson, c. 1955.
Intended for multiple seating arrangements, offered
with ganging option; oak face, maple core veneer
frame.
H 32", W 21", D 23"
Courtesy Thonet

Thonet
No. 1294 Molded Plywood Chair
Designed by Bruno Weill, c. 1945.
Inspired by the Eames "Potato Chip" Chair; oak
face, maple core veneer molded plywood leg
frames, back supports, seats and backs; optional
upholstered seat/back.
H 30", W 18", D 21"
Courtesy Thonet

Herman Miller (Herman Miller for the Home)
Eames Molded Plywood Chair (DCW)
Designed by Charles and Ray Eames, 1946.
Light ash face veneers and maple inner plies; five-ply seat and back, eight-ply
legs and lumbar support; clear coat or ebony; rubber shock mounts.
H 28-3/4", W 19-3/8", D 21-3/4"
Courtesy Herman Miller

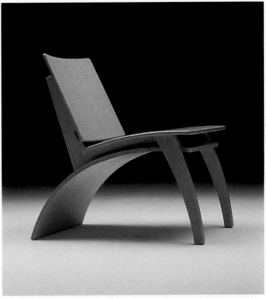

Design America
Blair Lounge Chair
Designed by Scott Blair c. 1990.
Molded cherry or ash plywood
chair with continuous back leg.
H 27", W 20", D 26"
Courtesy Design America

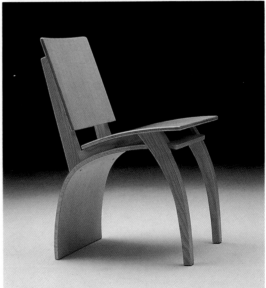

Design America
Blair Dining Chair
Designed by Scott Blair c.1990.
Molded cherry or ash plywood
chair with continuous back leg.
H 30-1/2", W 17", D 20"
Courtesy Design America

Thonet
No. 1216/18 Side Chair
Designed by Bruno Weill, c. 1945.
Thonet's first mass-produced bent plywood chair has remained in the product line since
1945; oak face, maple core veneer molded ply leg frame, back support, and back.
H 32", W 15", D 19"
Courtesy Thonet

15

Palazzetti
Chair
Designed by Carlo Bugatti, 1902.
Originally produced in Bugatti's workshop in Milan; eight made for his own dining room; adaptation of natural mahogany or black lacquered ash, seat and back covered in white goat parchment.
H 45-1/4", W 17-3/4", D 18-7/8"
Courtesy Palazzetti

Tendo
Chair
Designed by Daisaku Choh, 1960.
Low chair of Japanese oak veneered plywood; two canted J-shape supports with runners prevent damage to tatami mats; upholstered seat and back.
H 25-1/2", W 21-3/4", D 26-1/4"
Courtesy Tendo

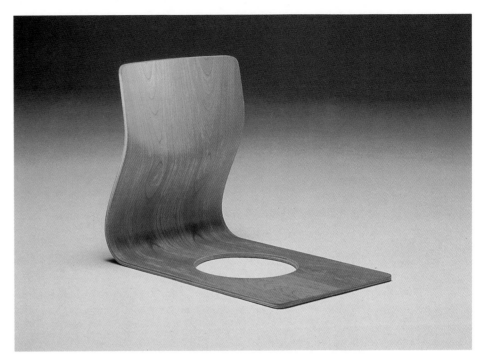

Top left: Tendo
Za Chair
Designed by Kenzo Tarumi, 1961.
Legless seat of curved plywood, Keyaki seat and back upholstered.
H 18-1/2", W 20-7/8", D 25-3/8"
Courtesy Tendo

Top right: Tendo
Chair
Designed by Kenji Fujimori, 1961.
Legless seat made of light bent plywood shell, designed to be stacked and stored in small spaces.
H 15-3/4", W 13", D 19-1/4"
Courtesy Tendo

Bottom left: Tendo
Za Chair
Designed by Yoshiteru Hara, 1982.
Legless seat of curved plywood, Saperi stained in black.
H 17", W 19-5/8", D 24"
Courtesy Tendo

Tendo
Spoke Chair
Designed by Katsuhei Toyoguchi, 1963.
Mid-height seat enables conversation with someone sitting on the floor; long fan-shaped back with vertical supports, made of oak, with upholstered seat.
H 32-3/4", W 31-1/2", D 26-1/4"
Courtesy Tendo

Alivar (available through Palazzetti)
Side Chair
Designed by Charles Rennie Mackintosh, 1904.
Originally commissioned by Miss Cranston of Glasgow; reproduction of black lacquered ash with stained glass inserts; seat upholstered in fabric or leather.
H 32", W 21-1/2", D 21"
Courtesy Palazzetti

Alivar (available through Palazzetti)
Armchair
Designed by Charles Rennie Mackintosh, 1904.
Taller version with arms.
H 49-1/2", W 21-1/2", D 21"
Courtesy Palazzetti

Tendo
Marilyn Chair
Designed by Arata Isozaki, 1972.
Black finish and narrow back emphasize the chair's vertical form, recalling designs by Mackintosh, while the curves represent Marilyn Monroe; first made by ICF and then Sunar in Canada, it has been produced by Tendo since 1981.
H 55-1/8", W 21-1/4", D 21-1/2"
Courtesy Tendo

Vitra
Schizzo
Designed by Ron Arad, 1989.
Molded plywood joined with steel tube; can be used as single chairs or combined to form a bench.
H 35", W 14-1/2", D 22-3/4"
Photo Hans Hansen, Courtesy Vitra

Smith & Hawken
Hampton Folding Chair
Outdoor chair of solid teak, with contoured back and seat, slats to shed rain, folds for storage in a 4" space, available with arms.
H 39-1/2", W 18-1/2, D 17"
Courtesy Smith & Hawken

20

Cassina
Ingram Chair (medium)
Designed by Charles Rennie
Mackintosh, 1900.
Originally oak stained dark with
horsehair upholstered seat, used
in the White Dining Room of the
Ingram Street Tea Rooms, 43
surviving examples.
H 41-3/4", seat 18-7/8" x 17-1/4"
Courtesy Cassina

Cassina
Ingram High Chair
Designed by Charles Rennie
Mackintosh, 1900.
Taller version of dining chair also
made for the White Dining Room,
but it is not known exactly where
these were used, four known
surviving examples of original.
H 59-3/4", seat 19" x 17-1/4"
Courtesy Cassina

Cassina
Ingram High Chair (with G.S.A Table)
Courtesy Cassina

22

Cassina
Argyle Tea Room Chair
Designed by Charles Rennie Mackintosh, 1897.
Originally dark stained (ebonized) oak, horsehair
upholstery on seat, which narrows toward the
back, with front legs tapering toward the bottom,
and front and side legs connected with pairs of
thin circular stretchers.
H 53-1/2", seat 19-3/4" x 18"
Courtesy Cassina

Cassina
Hill House Ladderback Chair
Designed by Charles Rennie Mackintosh, 1902-04.
Originally of ebonized oak with upholstered seat,
one of two chairs not painted white for the
bedroom of the Hill House; reissue of ebonized
ash wood.
H 55-1/2", seat H 17-3/4", base W 16-1/8",
D 13-3/4"
Courtesy Cassina

Shaker Workshops
No. 5 Shawl Back Side Chair
The Shakers were among the first in America to produce chairs on a large
scale, and the first of these were sold in Mount Lebanon, New York in 1776.
H 40 3/4", W 20 3/4"
Courtesy Shaker Workshops

Cassina
Superleggera
Designed by Gio Ponti, c. 1955.
Super lightweight chair, originally pro-
duced by Cassina in 1957; ash wood frame
with natural finish and cane seat.
H 32-5/8", W 16-1/8", D 18-1/2"
Courtesy Cassina

Tendo
Chair
Designed by Toshimitsu Sasaki, 1986.
Curved beech plywood stained black,
upholstered seat.
H 31-5/8", W 18-1/8", D 19-7/8"
Courtesy Tendo

ICF
Layered Wood Chair
Designed by Timothy deFiebre, 1993.
Frame of solid maple in a variety of
finishes, back of maple with triple-ply
insert, seat solid maple or foam
cushioned and upholstered; stacks 5
high.
H 32", W 19-3/4", D 21-1/2"
Courtesy ICF

Cassina
D.S.3 Chair
Designed by Charles Rennie Mackintosh,
1918.
Reissue of ebonized frame inlaid with
mother-of-pearl, sea-grass seat.
H 29-1/4", seat 19-1/8" x 17-1/2"
Courtesy Cassina

Brayton (Steelcase Design Partnership)
Eclipse
Designed by Professor Otto Votteler, c. 1989.
Wood stacking chair in arm or armless version: solid European beech frame with mortise and tenon and dowel joinery; seat and back of molded beech veneer; optional upholstery; stack up to 12 high.
H 32-1/4", W 19-3/4" or 32-1/4", D 21-1/4"
Courtesy Steelcase

Vecta (Steelcase Design Partnership)
Opera
Designed by Gerd Lange.
Stackable armchair or armless chair with frame of oval tubular steel; seat and back shell of textured polypropylene or finished maple; plastic arms; options include upholstery, ganging, and tablet arm.
H 30-3/4", W 24-1/2", D 21-1/2"
Courtesy Steelcase

Cassina
Midway 1 Chair
Designed by Frank Lloyd Wright, 1914.
The hexagonal-backed side chair with upholstered seat and back was designed for use in
the dining room of Midway Gardens in Chicago in 1914. Reissue frame of cherry wood,
natural or stained walnut, or black.
H 34-1/4", W 20-1/4", D 18-7/8"
Courtesy Cassina

Midway 1 Chair
Back view.
Courtesy Cassina

26

Vitra
Ota Otanek
Designed by Borek Sipek,
1988.
Armchair with lacquered
metal and turned wood
legs, solid wood seat,
hammered copper
backrest.
H 29-1/2", W 21-1/2",
D 25-1/2"
Courtesy Vitra

Tecta
Arm Chair
Designed by Stefan
Wewerka, 1979.
Three-legged chair with
curved back extending into
arms, lacquered
beechwood frame,
upholstered seat.
H 29-1/4", W 26-3/4", D 19"
Courtesy Tecta

Tendo
Chair
Designed by Yoshihiko
Terahara, 1992.
Asymmetrical three-legged
chair with back extending
down into leg; curved
beech plywood stained
black, seat upholstered.
H 32-1/4", W 18-1/8",
D 19-7/8"
Courtesy Tendo

Tendo
Child's Chair
Designed by Toshimitsu
Sasaki, 1980.
Wide U-shape base for
stability, extra rung as
footrest or to climb into
the seat, horseshoe-shape
front supports serve as
rockers when the chair is
turned over; made of
beech.
H 31", W 16-3/4",
D 19-1/2"
Courtesy Tendo

Vitra
Documenta Chair
Designed by Paolo Deganello.
Steel tube base with aluminum; turquoise woven wicker seat; black leather-covered
flexible back; yellow plastic leg.
H 41-1/2″, W 25-1/2″, D 21-1/2″
Courtesy Vitra

Knoll (Studio)
Cross Check Arm Chair
Designed by Frank O. Gehry, 1992.
Arm chair of 2-inch wide hard white maple strips of 6, 7, or 8-ply laminated veneers with
wood grain running in the same direction for resilience; with 1-inch thick foam seat cushion.
H 33-5/8″, W 28-1/2″, D 24-7/8″.
Courtesy Knoll

28

Knoll (Studio)
Gehry Collection
Designed by Frank O. Gehry, 1989-1992.
Power Play Club Chair with Off Side Ottoman, High Sticking High Back Chair, Hat Trick Arm Chair, Face Off Cafe
Table, and Cross Check Arm Chair: of 2-inch wide hard white maple strips of 6, 7, or 8-ply laminated veneers with
wood grain running in the same direction for resilience.
Courtesy Knoll

Cassina
Revers
Designed by Andrea
Branzi, c. 1993.
Chair with metallized
gray lacquered alumi-
num support structure,
curved beech plywood
seat; curved strip of
solid beechwood forms
back and armrests;
fabric upholstered foam
seat.
H 30", W 25-1/4", D 20"
Courtesy Cassina

Cassina
Revers
Designed by Andrea
Branzi, c. 1993.
Group of chairs without
upholstered seat.
Courtesy Cassina

Herman Miller (Herman
Miller for the Home)
**Eames Molded Plywood
Side Chair (DCM)**
Designed by Charles and
Ray Eames in 1946.
One of the most signifi-
cant chair designs of the
century: five-ply molded
plywood; hardwood
inner plies and light ash
face veneers with either
clear coat or ebony
finish; bright chrome-
plated steel rod base,
legs, and back brace;
rubber shock mounts;
nylon glides.
H 29-1/2", W 20-1/2"
Courtesy Herman Miller

ICF
Ant Chair
Designed by Arne
Jacobsen, 1952.
After its first showing
in 1952 it was named
Ant Chair for its
pinched waist and
thin legs. Molded
laminated natural
wood with beech or
maple veneer,
lacquered in 16
colors, chrome-
plated tubular steel
legs, black nylon feet.
H 30-1/2", W 19", D
19"
Courtesy ICF

30

Memphis
First
Designed by Michele De Lucchi in 1983.
Chair in metal and wood, comprised of a
stool with circular arm/back form and
circular backrest.
H 35-1/2", W 23-1/4", D 19-3/4"
Courtesy Memphis

Zero U.S.
Jessica
Designed by Donato D'Urbino & Paolo
Lomazzi, c. 1992.
Chair frame and legs of a single curved
steel wire, double back of translucent
polypropylene, upholstered seat.
H 31", W 18"
Courtesy Zero U.S.

Cassina
Midway 2 Chair
Designed by Frank Lloyd Wright, 1914.
The disc-shaped steel-rod side chair was
designed for the outdoor garden court of
Chicago's Midway Gardens in 1914;
reissue frame in glossy white, red, blue, or
gray enameled steel rod.
H 34-1/2", W 15-3/4", D 18-1/2"
Courtesy Cassina

Zero U.S.
Spring
Designed by Jonathan De Pas, Donato
D'Urbino & Paolo Lomazzi.
Chair base of black soft coated steel;
back base of harmonic steel; seat and
back of natural beechwood or
upholstered.
H 32", D 17"
Courtesy Zero U.S.

Tecta
B 80 Highback Chair
Designed by Jean Prouvé, 1928.
Folding chair with nickel-finish sheet metal
frame and removable seat cushion.
H 40-1/2", W 17-3/4", D 20"
Courtesy Tecta

Tecta
B 5 Cantilever Chair
Designed by Stefan Wewerka, 1982.
First single-leg cantilever chair; chromed
tubular steel frame in one continuous piece
with tubular backrest and saddle seat
covered in fabric or leather and attached to
the frame, giving the effect of a piece of
abstract art.
H 31-1/8", W 24-1/2", D 21-1/4"
Courtesy Tecta

Zero U.S.
Umbrella Chair
Designed by Gaetano Pesce.
Unique alternative to the folding chair, collapsible chair with gas spring movement; of
anodized drawn aluminum; seat, handle, joints, and feet of polypropylene and nylon
reinforced with glass fiber.
H 31-7/8", closed DM 6-1/4"; open W 17-3/4", D 19-1/4"
Courtesy Zero U.S.

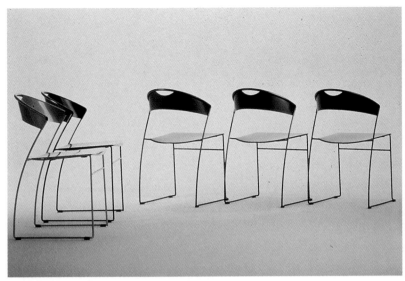

Baleri Italia (available through Luminaire)
Juliette
Designed by Hannes Wettstein.
Stackable chair with steel bar structure, painted stamped sheet steel seat and back; outdoor version of stainless steel.
H 30-1/3", W 17-3/4", D 19-1/4"
Courtesy Luminaire

Kartell (available through Luminaire)
Dr. Glob
Designed by Philippe Starck, c. 1989.
Stacking chair with steel tubing frame, polypropylene seat, available in several color combinations.
H 28-3/4", W 19", D 18-3/4"
Courtesy Luminaire

Alias (available through Luminaire)
Frame
Designed by Alberto Meda, c. 1991.
Chair with aluminum frame and molded plywood seat; open back reminiscent of Victorian balloon-back chair.
H 31/4", W 17-3/4", D 21-1/4"
Courtesy Luminaire

Palazzetti
Antelope Chair
Designed by Ernest Race,
1951.
Considered one of the best
British post-war designs, part
of the outdoor furniture line
Race designed for the 1951
Festival of Britain; frame of
bent steel wire lacquered in
black or white PVC, spherical
feet of lacquered brass,
Baydur seat.
H 31-1/2", W 21-5/8", D 23"
Courtesy Palazzetti

Arc Age
Shab Raffia Arm Chair
Designed by Behshad
Shokouhi, c. 1994.
Curved steel arms
extending to curved
and twisted front legs,
splayed back legs with
wood slat back,
upholstered seat.
H 31", W 22", D 24"
Courtesy Arc Age

Arc Age
Shab Arm Chair
Designed by Behshad
Shokouhi, c. 1994.
Curved steel arms extending
to curved and twisted front
legs, splayed back legs with
wood slat back and seat.
H 32", W 22", D 24"
Courtesy Arc Age

Arc Age
**Shab Arm Chair &
Foot Stool**
Designed by Behshad
Shokouhi, c. 1994.
Curved steel arms
extending to curved
and twisted front legs,
splayed back legs with
wood slat back and
seat. Footstool with
twisted steel legs and
wood slat top.
Stool H 15", W 17", D
15"
Courtesy Arc Age

Top left: Arc Age
Side Chair
Designed by Behshad Shokouhi, c. 1994.
Steel frame with wood slat back and seat.
Courtesy Arc Age

Center left: Arc Age
Doble Dining Chair
Designed by Behshad Shokouhi, c. 1994.
Curved steel back legs and backrest
support, straight front legs, upholstered
seat/back.
H 32", W 16", D 18"
Courtesy Arc Age

Top right: Arc Age
"Ghamish" Chair
Designed by Behshad Shokouhi, c. 1994.
Curved steel back legs, curved and
twisted backrest support and front legs,
upholstered seat/back.
H 32", W 16", D 18"
Courtesy Arc Age

Bottom left: Arc Age
Doble Armed Chair
Designed by Behshad Shokouhi, c. 1994.
Curved steel arms, back legs, and
backrest support, straight steel front legs,
upholstered seat/back and armrests.
H 32", W 24", D 20"
Courtesy Arc Age

Bottom center: Arc Age
Moft Classic Chair
Designed by Behshad Shokouhi, c. 1994.
Gently splayed steel back and legs, wood
backrest, upholstered seat/back.
H 31", W 17", D 19"
Courtesy Arc Age

Bottom right: Arc Age
Shab Nam Arm Chair
Designed by Behshad Shokouhi, c. 1994.
Curved steel arms extending to curved
and twisted front legs, splayed back legs
with upholstered seat/back.
H 31", W 22", D 24"
Courtesy Arc Age

Alias (available through Luminaire)
Spaghetti
Designed by Giandomenico Belotti, 1982.
Stacking armchair of tubular steel with horizontal plastic spaghetti strips forming seat and backrest.
H 33", W 21-1/4", D 20"
Courtesy Luminaire

ICF
Spaghetti Lounge Chair
Designed by Giandomenico Belotti, c. 1982.
Stacking lounge chair of chromed or baked epoxy finish steel frame; seat and back in colored spaghetti strips of PVC.
H 28", W 27", D 25"
Courtesy ICF

Alias (available through Luminaire)
High Frame
Designed by Alberto Meda, c. 1991.
Stacking chair of extruded aluminum profile and die-cast aluminum elements; black or silver frame, colored seat.
H 32-1/4", W 19-1/4", D 21-1/4"
Courtesy Luminaire

Driade (available through Luminaire)
Olly Tango
Designed by Philippe Starck.
Stackable chair of curved plywood
on chromium plated metal frame.
H 35-1/2", W 16-1/2", D 23"
Courtesy Luminaire

Knoll (Studio)
Handkerchief Stacking Arm Chair
Designed by Vignelli Designs, 1985.
Seat and back shell of woven rattan;
also available of compression-molded
fiberglass-reinforced polyester; non-
upholstered chairs stack 25 high.
H 29", W 26", D 22-1/2"
Courtesy Knoll

Driade (available through Luminaire)
Abanica
Stackable side chairs of anodized aluminum in light bronze finish; seat and
back in light brown rattan.
H 34-1/4", W 20-1/2", D 21-7/8"
Courtesy Luminaire

Bottom left: Alias (available through
Luminaire)
Armframe
Designed by Alberto Meda, c. 1991.
Armchair of extruded aluminum profile
and die-cast aluminum elements with
polyester net seat.
H 28-3/4", W 21-1/4", L 35-3/4"
Courtesy Luminaire

Bottom right: Artifort
Zeno
Designed by Wolfgang C.R. Mezger.
Stackable chair, with or without arms
and/or upholstery, can be linked
together or made as a beam-system;
armrests of plastic or beechwood,
aluminum base.
H 31-7/8", W 19-1/2" or 22", D 21-5/8"
Courtesy Artifort

37

Vitra
Louis 20
Stacked.
Courtesy Vitra

Vitra
Louis 20
Designed by Philippe Starck, 1991.
Multipurpose stacking chair made of blow-molded polypropylene to
achieve mass without weight; rear legs and arms of natural polished
aluminum; recyclable, for indoor or outdoor use.
H 33", W 23-1/2", D 23"
Courtesy Vitra

Vitra
Panton Chair
Designed by Verner Panton, 1960.
Originally produced by Vitra in 1968 under the Herman Miller label. Single-piece molded
plastic stacking chair in primary colors or neutral; indoor/outdoor use.
H 33-1/2", W 19-3/4", D 21-1/2"
Courtesy Vitra

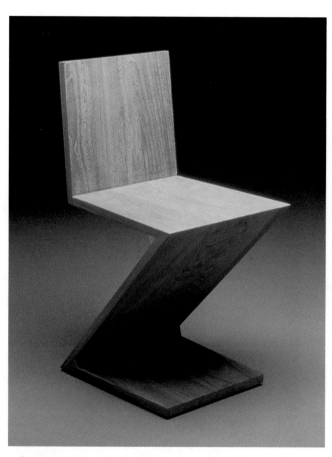

Cassina
Zig-Zag Chair
Designed by Gerrit T. Rietveld, 1934.
Unique chair design; construction uses dovetailing and nuts
and bolts; in 1971 Cassina acquired the rights to reproduce
all Rietveld furniture; reissued in finished or unfinished edge-
grain laminated elm.
H 29-1/8", seat H 17", base W 14-1/2", D 17"
Courtesy Cassina

Vitra
Easy Edges Side Chair (with Dining Table)
Designed by Frank O. Gehry, 1972/92.
Approx. 50 layers of corrugated cardboard with edges finished in hardboard.
Chair H 32-1/4", W 14-1/4", D 21-1/2"; Table H 29", L 78-3/4", W 35-1/2"
Courtesy Vitra

40

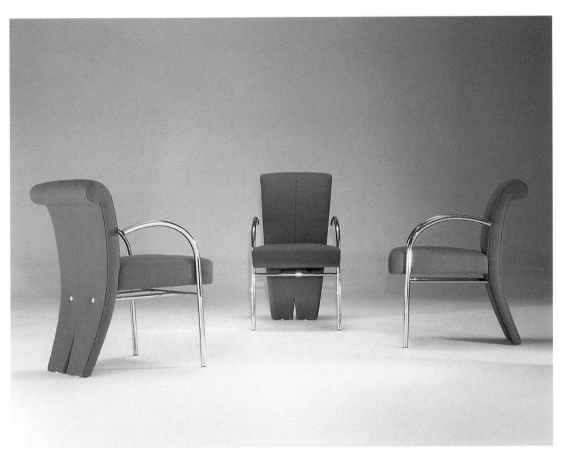

Brueton Industries
Tux High & Low Back
Designed by Stanley Jay Friedman, 1993.
Polished or satin tubular steel frame, leather or
fabric upholstered seat and back, the back and
back legs in the form of coat tails extending to the
floor.
H 32 & 36", W 20", D 27 & 28"
Courtesy Brueton

Vitra
Greene Street
Designed by Gaetano Pesce, 1984.
Seat and back of black plastic with
three cutout holes; eight metal rod legs
ending in plastic feet, resembling an
insect.
H 37-1/2", W 21"
Courtesy Vitra

Halifax (available through Luminaire)
Minni
Designed by Antonio Citterio.
Seating system in which the basic structure, of polyamide reinforced with fiberglass, supports various components -- legs, seat, back, arm rests; legs and arm rests of anodized aluminum or solid beechwood; seat of polypropylene; all plastics are 100% recyclable.
H 31-1/2", W 18-1/2" or 20-2/3", D 20"
Courtesy Luminaire

Thonet
Attiva Stacking Chair
Designed by Jerome Caruso, c. 1990.
High density stack chair system with "flex" movement of wire frame and plastic shell, compound curve for ergonomic support; side, arm, upholstery, tablet arm, and ganging options.
H 31" or 32", W 20-3/4" to 23-1/2", D 22"
Courtesy Thonet

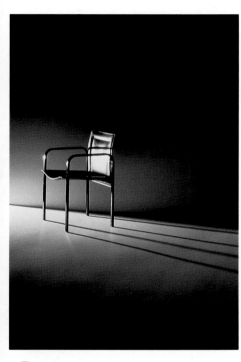

Thonet
Stuva Chair
Designed by Studio Arrben, c, 1990.
Made of only four parts; oval tubular steel
frame with leather seat and back.
H 32", W 22", D 22"
Courtesy Thonet

Thonet
Sof-Tech Side Chair
Designed by David Rowland, c. 1979.
Plastic-coated spring material on seat and
back gives transparent effect; 7/8" diameter
14 gauge tubular steel frames with minimal
parts for mass production.
H 29-3/4", W 19-3/4", D 20-1/2"
Courtesy Thonet

Driade (available through Luminaire)
Irta
Designed by Jorge Pensi.
Stackable armchair with anodized aluminum tubular frame, die-cast and shot-blasted
aluminum seat and back with indoor version coated with blue felt.
H 32-1/4", W 22-1/16", D 20-1/2"
Courtesy Luminaire

Knoll (Studio)
Toledo Stacking Chairs (with Table)
Designed by Jorge Pensi, 1988.
Seat, back, and arms of polished cast aluminum; legs of anodized polished tubular
aluminum; stack up to 8 high.
H 29-7/8", W 21-5/8", D 21-1/4"
Courtesy Knoll

44

Thonet
Alisea Chair
Designed by Studio Simonetti, c. 1990.
Stacking chair with polished cast aluminum frame and molded aluminum back.
H 31", W 20", D 19-1/2"
Courtesy Thonet

Smith & Hawken
Toscano Armchair (with Salerno Square Table)
Tubular steel with powder-coat finish, slatted back and seat, stackable chair. Table of
industrial grade sheet metal with polyester finish.
Chair H 33", W 20", D 20"; table H 29", DM 30"
Courtesy Smith & Hawken

Smith & Hawken
Galvanized Chair
Based on a 1926 design of a "French Terrace Chair"; treated in
a zinc bath to create a pleasing spangled texture while
rendering them rust resistant; sturdy and stackable, with seat
holes to disperse rain; made in France.
H 33-1/2", W 17-3/8", D 18"
Courtesy Smith & Hawken

Top left: Thonet
Lorenz Chair
Designed by Anton Lorenz, c. 1930.
A reinterpretation of the Luckhardt chair, designed by Anton Lorenz, the founder of a small furniture factory in Desta. Thonet purchased Desta in 1932 and acquired all design rights. Made of 1" diameter 13 gauge tubular steel frame and elastic strap seat base, with foam in upholstered seat and back.
H 29", W 23-1/2", D 22"
Courtesy Thonet

Top right: Palazzetti
Chair
Designed by Oliver Percy Bernard, 1931.
Similar to the Luckhardt Chair of 1928, with a thinner seat. Bernard designed this version for Pel in 1931, and in 1982 it was reintroduced by Sheridan Coakley. Frame of mirror-polished chrome-plated steel tube or with black epoxy finish; seat with hardwood frame, elastic webbing, and fabric or leather-covered foam; arms and back hardwood frame and upholstered foam.
H 29-3/4", W 21", D 24"
Courtesy Palazzetti

Bottom left: Thonet
B302 Revolving Chair
Designed by Charlotte Perriand, c. 1928.
Charlotte Perriand, one of Le Corbusier's colleagues, exhibited at the Salon des Artistes Décorateurs and unveiled the revolving chair in her dining room. More of a reinterpretation of the past than a revolutionary statement, the form expressed overtones of the Thonet bentwood B9 chair, which Le Corbusier was very fond of using. Perriand reduced the cold tubular steel quality by adding padded components. It was manufactured by Gebrüder Thonet after 1929; currently of 1" diameter 14 gauge polished chrome plated tubular steel frame, upholstered foam padded seat and backrest, covered in standard black leather.
H 28-1/2", W 24-1/2", D 22"
Courtesy Thonet

Bottom right: Thonet
Luckhardt Chair
Designed by Hans and Wassili Luckhardt, c. 1929.
Side Chair Model No. ST14 of bent chromed tubular steel and plywood was designed by two brothers from Berlin who were influential in German expressionist architecture, Wassili Luckhardt (1899-1972) and Hans Luckhardt (1890-1954). It was manufactured by Desta in 1931, and Thonet acquired the company in 1932; currently of 1" diameter 14 gauge tubular steel frame with upholstered foam padded seat and back.
H 33", W 21", D 23"
Courtesy Thonet

Opposite page:
Top left: Thonet
Stam Chair
Designed by Mart Stam, c. 1926-27.
Although Stam is credited with inventing the cantilever principle, which was first seen at the Weissenhof exhibition in Stuttgart, c. 1929, Breuer may have actually preceded him. The design is also significant for its departure from the four-legged chair. Adaptation of Stam original design made of 1" diameter 14 gauge polished chrome plated tubular steel frame, with oak veneer molded plywood seat and back, exposed fasteners, solid oak armrests.
Arm Chair: H 30-3/8"; W 20-1/2", D 19-1/2"; Side Chair W 16"
Courtesy Thonet

Top right: Thonet
Classic Breuer "Cesca" Chair
Designed by Marcel Breuer, c. 1928.
Breuer was the first to successfully combine these three materials and also introduced a non-continuous frame on a cantilevered chair with a back support curved or bent on the vertical plane. It was named Cesca after his daughter Francesca. The original side and seat rails were made from a rod of solid wood bent into a C shape secured by a straight front rail. After World War II the seat frames were made from four pieces of wood joined together. It was made by Gebrüder Thonet beginning in 1931.
Side Chair, cane or upholstered seat, H 32", W 18-1/4", D 22-1/2"; Arm Chair W 23".
Courtesy Thonet

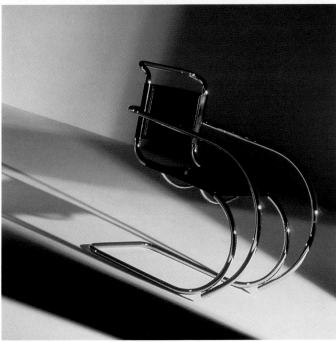

Bottom left: Thonet
MR534 Mies Arm Chair
Designed by Ludwig Mies van der Rohe, c. 1927.

Introduced in the same year as Stam's, and the only other cantilever design shown at the 1927 Stuttgart exhibit sponsored by the Deutsche Werkbund under the artistic direction of its vice-president Mies van der Rohe, this design is considered to be the most graceful of the early cantilevered chairs. Originally Model No. MR10 of bent nickeled tubular steel, cane, bent solid steel, and wood, it was produced by two firms in Berlin and then by Thonet from 1932, when it became referred to as MR533 and MR533g with woven cane seat. The lightweight design provided resiliency and easy movement in modest living areas for low-income residents. Currently made of 1" diameter 11 gauge polished chrome plated tubular steel frame with black leather upholstery.
Side Chair H 33", W 19", D 28"; Arm Chair H 34", W 22", D 32"
Courtesy Thonet

Bottom right: Knoll
MR Arm Chair
Designed by Mies van der Rohe, c. 1927.
Chrome plated tubular steel frame, shown with woven rattan upholstery.
H 31", W 21", D 32-1/2"
Courtesy Knoll

Tecta
MR Chair
Designed by Mies van der Rohe, c. 1927.
Armless version with chrome plated tubular steel frame and woven rattan upholstery.
H 31″, W 18-7/8″, D 29-1/8″
Courtesy Tecta

Tecta
B 20 Chair
Designed by Jean Prouvé, patented by Tecta 1987.
Stackable chair with cantilevered tubular steel frame with woven seat and back in a variety of colors; optional seat cushion.
H 35″, W 19-5/8″, D 22″
Courtesy Tecta

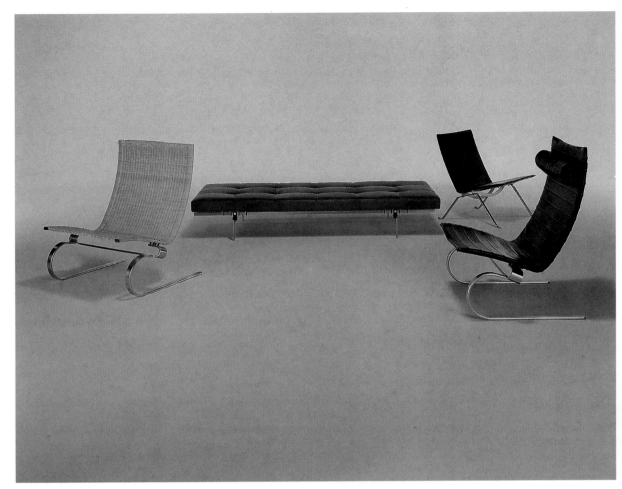

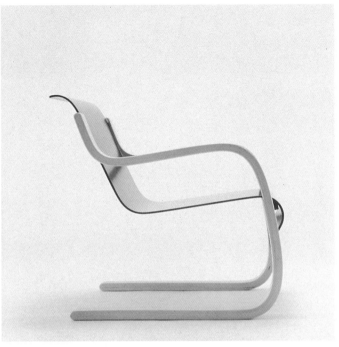

ICF
Kjaerholm Collection
Designed by Poul Kjaerholm, 1956-1979.
Lounge Chair, Low-back Lounge Chair, High-back
Lounge Chair with removable headrest, and Bench:
frame of chromium-plated spring steel; chairs uphol-
stered in leather, lounge also in canvas or natural wicker.
H 28" or 35", W 25" or 31-1/2", D 25", 26-3/4", or 30";
bench H 12", W 31-1/2", L 70-3/4"
Courtesy ICF

Top right: ICF
Aalto Unupholstered Lounge Chair
Designed by Alvar Aalto, 1932.
Natural birch frame; seat and back of lacquered birch.
H 28", W 24", D 28-1/2"
Courtesy ICF

Bottom right: ICF
Aalto Pension Chair
Designed by Alvar Aalto, 1946.
Cantilevered frame of natural birch, seat and back of
linen webbing.
H 33", W 23-5/8", D 28-1/4"
Courtesy ICF

Thonet
B55 Arm Chair
Designed by Marcel Breuer, c. 1928.
Another early variation of Breuer's
cantilever designs. Adaptation of
B55 Arm Chair with black leather
seat and back; currently made of 1"
diameter 14 gauge tubular steel
frame with standard black leather
seat and back slings.
H 33", W 19-5/8", D 25-1/2"
Courtesy Thonet

Thonet
B34 Arm Chair
Designed by Marcel Breuer, c. 1933.
Breuer's continuous version of the
cantilever concept with a stretch fabric
seat and back eliminated the need for
traditional upholstery techniques.
Currently of 1" diameter 13 gauge
polished chrome plated tubular steel
frame, standard black leather seat and
back slings, black leather arm rests.
H 31", W 22", D 23"
Courtesy Thonet

Thonet
Brno Chair
Designed by Ludwig Mies van der
Rohe, c. 1930.
This was designed for the dining
area of a house overlooking Brno,
Czechoslovakia that was commissioned by Grete and Fritz Tugendhat
in 1928. The Tugendhat House is best
known for the harmonious relationship between van der Rohe's
architecture and interior furnishings.
Thonet acquired the rights to this
design in 1932. Made of 1" diameter
13 gauge tubular steel frame with
upholstered foam cushion in seats
and backs.
H 29-1/2", W 22", D 24-1/2"
Courtesy Thonet

Knoll (Studio)
Brno Chair
Tubular stainless steel or chrome
plated steel with leather upholstery,
part of the Knoll Studio Mies van der
Rohe Collection.
H 31-1/2", W 22-3/4", D 22-1/2"
Courtesy Knoll

Thonet
Brno Barstock Chair
Designed by Mies van der Rohe, c. 1930.
Brno flat bar stainless steel chair with arm pads, originally designed in 1929 by Mies van der Rohe for his house in Brno, Czechoslovakia. It was first manufactured in Berlin and then by Thonet from 1932, after acquiring design rights to produce Mies van der Rohe designs. Made of chromed flat barstock steel frame, leather upholstery.
H 32", W 22-1/2", D 25"
Courtesy Thonet

Thonet
Churchill Cantilever Chair
Designed by Thonet staff, c. 1931.
By the mid-thirties, many variations of tubular steel designs were offered in the Thonet catalog. This design was used in Winston Churchill's underground headquarters in London during World War II. Currently of 1" diameter 14 gauge tubular steel frame, upholstered foam-padded seat back and arms, plywood seat interior.
H 31-1/2", W 22-3/4", D 24"
Courtesy Thonet

Thonet
Stacking Breuer Chair
Designed by Thonet design staff, 1980.
Adaptation of 1928 Breuer design, 1" diameter 11 gauge tubular steel frame, beech or white oak seat/back frames, upholstered seat and back, stacks 5 high freestanding.
H 32", W 18-1/2", D 22-1/2"
Courtesy Thonet

Thonet
Interlock Stack Arm Chair
Designed by Warren Snodgrass, c. 1982.
Cantilever stackable chair with oval tubing and slim contoured upholstered one-piece seat and back for interlocking stack; steel frames with foam upholstered seat/back.
H 32-1/4", W 23", D 24"
Courtesy Thonet

Design America
Springer Chair
Designed by Richard Neutra c.1930s.
Cantilevered tubular steel chair with upholstered seat and back.
H 29-1/2", W 22", D 29"
Courtesy Design America

ICF
Cinema
Designed by Gunilla Allard.
Chair (also ottoman and lounge) of steel tube frame with powder coat or chrome finish, arms covered in leather, seat and back cushions upholstered in fabric or leather.
H 31", W 22", D 29-1/2"
Courtesy ICF

Thonet
Plaza Lounge
Designed by Fabio N. Fabiano, c. 1988.
Front leg/arm 16 gauge tubular steel
frame; rear leg support 2" tube; foam
padded seat over Futurestyle molded
plywood back.
H 29-3/4", W 31", D 23"
Courtesy Thonet

Artifort
Maxime
Designed by Carlos Castellanos.
Cantilevered chair (also made with
5-star swivel base for office use);
tubular frame, back of metal
covered in preformed foam, seat
preformed pressed beechwood
shell.
H 37-3/4", W 25-3/4", D 20-5/8"
Courtesy Artifort

Knoll (Studio)
Mandarin Chair
Designed by Sottsass Associati, 1986.
Tubular steel frame with detachable
legs in chrome or matte black finish,
bent rattan or tubular steel arms, seat
and back upholstered in fabric or
leather.
H 32-1/2", W 26", D 23-1/2"
Courtesy Knoll

Herman Miller (Herman Miller for the
Home)
Equa Rocker
Designed by Bill Stumpf and Don
Chadwick, 1984.
With flexible one-piece shell with H-
shaped cutout, thick foam padding,
waterfall edges, and rocker base; part
of the series of Equa swivel office
chairs.
H 35", W 25-1/2", D 16-3/4"
Courtesy Herman Miller

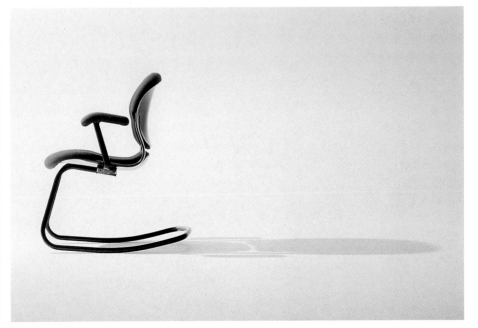

Thonet
Erbe Stacking Chair
Designed by Dorsey Cox, c. 1987.
Flexible design in stacking, ganging, tablet arm, handhold, and various color combinations and upholstery options; 13-gauge tubular steel frame.
H 33", W 21", D 23-1/2"
Courtesy Thonet

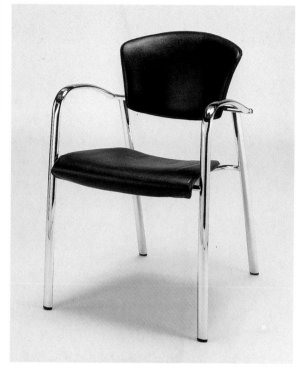

Brayton (Steelcase Design Partnership)
BCN
Designed by Josep Lluscà, c. 1983.
Stacking Armchair with frame of oval tubular steel finished in chrome, metallic, or black; contoured reinforced fiberglass seat and back upholstered in leather or fabric over foam.
H 31-3/4", W 20-3/4", D 24"
Courtesy Steelcase

Brayton (Steelcase Design Partnership)
Tonga
Designed by Burkhard Vogtherr.
Stacking armchair or armless versions of round tubular steel with powdercoat finish or maple veneer frame in 31 layers; round or square articulating back; upholstered in fabric or leather over foam; ganging option.
H 31-3/4", W 19-3/4" to 23", D 21-1/2"
Courtesy Steelcase

54

Thonet
Erbe Sled Base Chair
Designed by Dorsey Cox, c. 1987.
Sled option for easy gliding and movement.
H 33", W 19-3/4", D 23-3/4"
Courtesy Thonet

Palazzetti
"Non-conformist" Chair
Designed by Eileen Gray, 1926-1927.
Left arm eliminated for more flexible seating positions;
frame of chrome-plated tubular steel; seat and back
upholstered in fabric or leather.
H 30-1/4", W 17-1/2", D 19-1/4"
Courtesy Palazzetti

Tecta
B 40 Backrest Chair
Designed by Marcel Breuer, 1926.
Nickel-plated tubular steel frame with sled base; cloth attached to the frame forming minimal seat and backrest.
H 32-1/4", W 17-3/4", D 20"
Courtesy Tecta

ICF
Breuer Lounge Chair
Designed by Marcel Breuer, 1928.
Frame of chrome-plated steel tube; seat and back natural wicker or natural leather in black, brown, or natural.
H 32-1/2", W 25-1/2", D 31-1/2"
Courtesy ICF

Tecta
D 81 Lounge Chair
Designed by Jean Prouvé, 1927.
Lounge chair with metal frame in the form of two rectangles supporting the center seat section, covered in fabric with a cushion headrest.
H 33-1/2", W 26-3/8", D 37-3/8"
Courtesy Tecta

Thonet
B35 Lounge Chair
Designed by Marcel Breuer, c. 1928.
This achievement in tubular steel design was shown extensively at the
1930 Salon des Artists Décorateurs in the Deutsche Werkbund. It appears
to be constructed of one continuous piece of steel, enabling economical
production. The design introduces two cantilevers, giving it excellent
resiliency and bounce. Currently of 1" diameter 13 gauge tubular steel
frame, standard black leather seat and back slings (optional channel
upholstery), maple wood arms.
H 32-3/4", W 24", D 31-1/2"
Courtesy Thonet

Cassina
Red and Blue
Designed by Gerrit T. Rietveld, 1918.
Rietveld's original armchair was made of machined solid wood with the
frame joined by dowels; seat and back nailed to the frame, and stained. In
1923 he made a version in primary colors, which was mass-produced by
Cassina beginning in 1971: beechwood marine plywood frame with black
and yellow aniline finish, seat with blue lacquer finish, back in red lacquer
finish.
H 34-5/8", front seat H 13", base W 25-3/4", D 32-5/8"
Courtesy Cassina

Thonet
Bentwood Rocker
Designed by Michael Thonet, c. 1862.
Perhaps inspired by the Winfield rocker which combined legs and runners, first
exhibited at the Crystal Palace Exhibition in London in 1851, Michael Thonet used
his ingenious method to produce the first bentwood rocker shortly thereafter.
Various models were introduced in the 1850s and 1860s. Steambent wood frame
with natural cane seat and back.
H 43", W 21", D 40"
Courtesy Thonet

ICF
Scroll Chair
Designed by Alvar Aalto, 1929.
Designed for the Paimio Sanitarium, Aalto's classic chair is made entirely of
laminated bentwood; frame of natural laminated birch; seat and back lacquered
laminated birch.
H 25-1/4", W 23-5/8", D 33-1/2"
Courtesy ICF

Thonet
Wassily Chair
Designed by Marcel Breuer, c.1925.
Breuer was inspired by the form and materials of bicycles, and translated them into a revolutionary new chair. Early tubular metal prototypes made of nickeled steel required the aid of a plumber and were only theoretically suited for mass production. Original fabrics included canvas, leather, or Eisengarn (iron cloth) which could be used outdoors. Breuer named the chair thirty years later, after his artist friend Wassily Kandinsky, who also taught at the Bauhaus and was fond of the design. Gebrüder Thonet manufactured the chair after 1928. Polished chrome plated tubular steel frame; black leather seat, back, and arms.
H 28-1/2", W 31", D 26-1/2"
Courtesy Thonet

Knoll (Studio)
Wassily Chair
Designed by Marcel Breuer, c.1925.
H 29", W 31", D 27-1/2"
Courtesy Knoll

Tecta
D4 Bauhaus Chair
Designed by Marcel Breuer, 1927.
Canvas or leather seat, back and arm straps stretched on nickel-plated tubular steel frame for lightweight seating; folds for easy storage and portability.
H 28", W 30-5/8", D 24"
Courtesy Tecta

Thonet
B301 Armchair
Designed by Le Corbusier, c. 1929.
This bent and chromed tubular steel chair with fabric seat and back was manufactured by Gebrüder Thonet in 1929. Le Corbusier had reinterpreted an inexpensive wood campaign chair featuring a pivoting canvas seat and back that was retailed by Maples & Co. of London. However, because numerous models were made, and the joints were welded and finely finished, the chair was costly to produce and only affordable by the wealthy. Currently of 1" diameter 13 gauge tubular steel frame with standard black leather seat, stretched by elastic spirals.
H 26", W 24", D 24
Courtesy Thonet

Brayton (Steelcase Design Partnership)
Futu
Designed by Fuss Design, c. 1990.
Modular armchair or armless one to four-seater; tubular steel frame, chrome or powdercoat finishes, seat and back sprung with sheet webbing, with fabric or leather over foam.
H 32", W 25-3/4" or 26-1/2", D 29-1/4"
Courtesy Steelcase

Herman Miller
Eames Aluminum Group Lounge Chair & Ottoman
Designed by Charles and Ray Eames, 1958.
Available in choice of seven fabrics; upholstered headrest; polished die-cast aluminum five-star base, frame, and optional arms; tubular steel column with enamel finish; nylon suspension; 1/2-inch glides.
Lounge H 37", W 25-3/4", D 28-1/2"; ottoman H 18-1/4", top 21-1/2" x 21"
Courtesy Herman Miller

Herman Miller
Eames Aluminum Group Side Chair
Designed by Charles and Ray Eames, 1958.
Available in choice of seven fabrics; polished die-cast five-star aluminum base, frame, and optional arms; tubular steel column with enamel finish; layered vinyl cushioning and nylon suspension, swivel mechanism; 1/2" glides.
H 33-3/4" max, W 23", D 17"
Courtesy Herman Miller

Knoll (Studio)
Risom Armless Lounge Chair
Designed by Jens Risom, 1941.
Select clear maple hardwood in
clear finish, mortise and tenon
construction, upholstery of 2-inch
straps of cotton webbing.
H 29-3/4", W 20", D 28"
Courtesy Knoll

Knoll (Studio)
Risom Collection
Designed by Jens Risom, 1941.
Courtesy Knoll

Knoll (Studio)
Risom Side Chair
Designed by Jens Risom, 1941.
Select clear maple hardwood in clear
finish, mortise and tenon construction,
upholstery of 2-inch straps of cotton
webbing.
H 30-1/8", W 17-1/4", D 18"
Courtesy Knoll

Knoll (Studio)
Ricchio JR Chair
Designed by Joseph Ricchio, 1995.
Select clear maple hardwood in clear or stained finish; dowel
and mortise and tenon construction; 1-inch thick easily
removed seat cushion covered in fabric or leather.
H 32-1/8", W 23-1/2", D 21-5/8"
Courtesy Knoll

Knoll (Studio)
Ricchio JR Chair, Stacking
Designed by Joseph Ricchio, 1995.
H 32-1/8", W 23-1/2", D 21-5/8"
Courtesy Knoll

Knoll (Studio)
Ricchio JR Chair
Designed by Joseph Ricchio, 1995.
Ricchio Chairs with various finishes and
upholstery.
H 32-1/8", W 23-1/2", D 21-5/8"
Courtesy Knoll

63

Thonet
Mesa Chair
Designed by John
Caldwell, c. 1988.
Maple plywood
molded frame,
upholstered foam
padded seat and back
over Futurestyle
webbing.
H 32", W 23", D 25"
Courtesy Thonet

Thonet
Petitt Occasional
Designed by Don Petitt,
c. 1978.
Oak face and maple
core veneer molded
plywood frames;
molded foam in
upholstered seats and
backs over plastic
shells or integral metal
frame seat and back.
H 31-1/2", W 22", D 24"
Courtesy Thonet

Thonet
Petitt Stacking
Designed by Don
Petitt, c. 1986.
Oak face, maple core
veneer molded
plywood frame,
upholstered foam
seat/back, stacks 7
high.
H 31", W 21-1/2", D
23-1/2"
Courtesy Thonet

Thonet
Dolmas Stacking Chairs
Designed by Just
Bernhard Meijer, c.
1986.
Molded plywood frame
with polypropylene
plastic shell for light-
weight and durable
seating.
H 30-1/2", W 20-5/8", D
20-1/2"
Courtesy Thonet

64

ICF
Aalto Armchair
Designed by Alvar Aalto, 1929.
Natural birch frame, seat and back upholstered in fabric or
leather on foam cushion; stacks 3 high.
H 27-1/2", W 20-1/2", D 19-1/2"
Courtesy ICF

Design America
Knickerbocker Pullup Armchair, High Cafe Armchair, Conference Armchair
Designed by Gilbert Rohde, early 1930s.
Distinctive arm with Art Deco "three parallel lines"; of maple or cherry wood, fabric or Spinneybeck leather uphol-
stery.
H 32", 40-1/2", 32"; W 21", 22-1/2", 21"; D 23", 22", 23"
Courtesy Design America

Montis (available through Luminaire)
Dione
Designed by Gijs Papavoine.
Dining chair of maple with matching or contrasting seat and back upholstery.
H 33-3/4", W 18-3/4" without arms; H 33", W 21-3/4" with arms; D 22".
Courtesy Luminaire

66

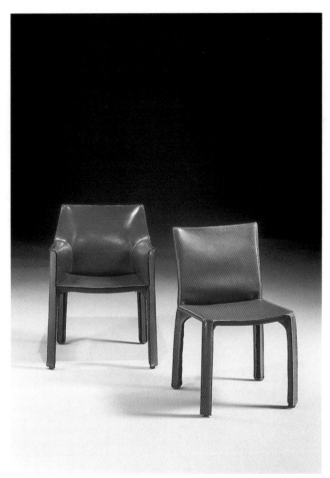

Cassina
Cos
Designed by Josep Lluscà.
From a collection of leather arm and side chairs for dining or conferencing; four-leg wood base, seat, back, and arms of steel-reinforced polyurethane, covered in saddle leather.
H 32-1/4" W 18-1/2", D 22-1/2"
Courtesy Cassina

Cassina
Cab
Designed by Mario Bellini, 1976.
Chair and armchair with steel frame, polyurethane padding and zippered saddle leather cover stretched over the entire frame.
H 32-1/4", W 20-1/2" and 23-5/8", D 18-1/2" and 20-1/2"
Courtesy Cassina

Cassina
Cab Armchair
Designed by Mario Bellini, 1976.
Armchair with steel frame, polyurethane padding and zippered saddle leather cover.
H 32-1/4", W 23-5/8", D 20-1/2"
Courtesy Cassina

Thonet
No. 1841 Arm Chair
Designed by Michael Thonet's sons, c. 1904.
A variation of the Gustav Siegal armchair, No. 715F-O, with a decorative cut out back; adaptation of steambent beechwood frame, upholstered foam padded seat.
H 29", W 22", D 21"
Courtesy Thonet

Thonet
Sunday
Designed by Jorge Pensi, c. 1990.
Elaborate slat back chair with steambent beechwood frame, stacks 5 freestanding.
H 32-1/2", W 22-3/4", D 20-1/2"
Courtesy Thonet

ICF
Layered Wood Armchair
Designed by Timothy deFiebre, 1993.
Frame of solid maple with black lacquer finish, back of maple with triple-ply insert, seat of solid maple or foam cushioned and upholstered; stacks 4 high.
H 32", W 23-1/2", D21-1/2"
Courtesy ICF

Thonet
Stoltz Arm Chair
Designed by Valtea Georg, c. 1990.
Comfort with minimal bentwood components; solid steambent beechwood frame, upholstered foam cushion seat/back.
H 31", W 22-1/2", D 22-1/2"
Courtesy Thonet

Top left: Haworth
Katia Chair
Spindle-back chair with maple frame with American cherry finish, upholstered seat.
H 31", W 24-1/8", D 23-1/2"
Courtesy Haworth

Bottom left: ICF
White Chair
Designed by Eliel Saarinen, c. 1910.
Hand-carved in Finnish Jugendstil style, the frame of solid birch lacquered pearl white; seat foam cushion upholstered with Seashell fabric designed by Irma Kukkasjarvi, or to specification.
H 32-7/8", W 26-3/4", D 21-1/4"
Courtesy ICF

Right: ICF
Blue Chair
Designed by Eliel Saarinen, 1929.
Art Deco inspired design with frame of solid birch, lacquered gray-blue with gold painted detail, seat upholstered in blue jacquard designed by Irma Kukkasjarvi, or to specification.
H 30", W 25", D 19-3/4"
Courtesy ICF

ICF
Villa Ast Chair
Designed by Josef Hoffmann, 1911.
Hoffmann's classic executive pull-up chair with geometric design; frame of ebonized or stained beech, seat upholstered in Josef Hoffmann fabrics or to specification.
H 32-1/2", W 23-5/8", D 21-1/4"
Courtesy ICF

Thonet
Hoffmann Chair
Designed by Josef Hoffmann, c. 1909.
As the Fledermaus Chair became a generic type, many variations evolved. Hoffmann designed this with a more accommodating scale and either a circular or diamond motif connecting the arm with the seat; steambent beechwood frame with upholstered seat.
H 29"; W 24", D 20-1/2", seat 18-1/2" x 19", arm H 29"
Courtesy Thonet

Thonet
Classic Corbusier Chair
Designed by Michael Thonet's sons, c. 1904.
The revival of the traditional Thonet bentwood furniture during the 1920s is attributed to Le Corbusier, who used it in his avant-garde interiors. He referred to this model as "the humble Thonet chair that possesses nobility." Adaptation of steambent beechwood frame, upholstered foam padded or natural cane seat and back.
H 31", W 21-1/2", D 22-1/2"
Courtesy Thonet

ICF
China Chair
Designed by Hans Wegner, 1944.
Danish classic of solid natural cherry or solid natural or stained mahogany, reversible seat pad in leather.
H 32-1/4", W 21-1/2", D 21-1/2"
Courtesy ICF

70

ICF
Hannes' Chair
Designed by Eliel Saarinen, 1908.
Saarinen designed this chair for the home of his brother Hannes in Finland. Frame of solid mahogany with rosewood insets; seat of foam padding covered in black leather with copper nailheads.
H 31-1/2", W 22", D 20-1/2"
Courtesy ICF

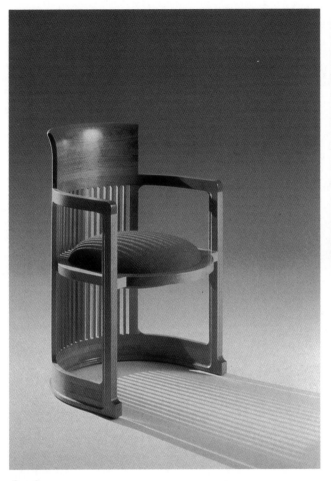

Cassina
Barrel Chair
Designed by Frank Lloyd Wright, 1937.
Wright designed the first version of this chair in oak for the Darwin Martin house in Buffalo, New York in 1904. This version of the armchair with curved back and upholstered seat was made for the Herbert Johnson house, Wing-spread, in Racine, Wisconsin in 1937. When Wright saw the completed chairs he ordered twelve for his own living room at Taliesen. Reissue in cherry wood or natural or stained walnut.
H 31-7/8", base W 21-1/2", D 21-7/8"
Courtesy Cassina

Thonet
Hoffmann Arm Chair
Designed by Thonet U.S.A. c. 1990.
Adaptation of Hoffmann designs employing nontraditional slats as back support; of steambent beechwood frame with bird's-eye maple back, upholstered seat cushion.
H 29", W 24", D 20-1/2"
Courtesy Thonet

Cassina
Willow Tea Room Chair
Designed by Charles
Rennie Mackintosh, 1903-
1904.
Curved lattice-back chair
of ebonized oak, not
actually circular, but
segmental with a stylized
willow tree in the grid
back; the bottom of the
seat serving as a small
locker or chest, used at the
order desk of the Willow
Tea Room.
H 46 3/4", W 37", D 15-3/4"
Courtesy Cassina

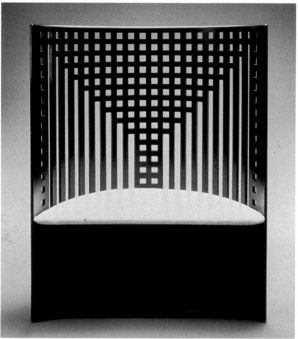

Cassina
Willow Tea Room Chair
Designed by Charles Rennie
Mackintosh, 1903-04.
Back view.
Courtesy Cassina

Thonet
Hoffmann Arm Chair
Designed by Josef Hoffmann,
c. 1908.
Adaptation of original
Hoffmann design; steambent
beechwood frame with
upholstered foam padded
seat.
H 31", W 22-1/2", D 20"
Courtesy Thonet

Tendo
Armchair
Designed by Shigeaki Seki,
1994.
Semi-circular chair with strips
of curved beech plywood
connecting the top rail and
base, stained black, seat with
upholstered cushion.
H 27-1/2", W 23-5/8", D 18-7/8"
Courtesy Tendo

72

Tecta
D 61 Armchair
Designed by El Lissitzky for the 1930 Dresden
Exhibition.
Barrel-shaped chair bent, black and blue
stained beech plywood; high armrests; seat
with open space beneath and leather back
cushion.
H 28-3/4", W 22-1/2", D 19-1/4"
Courtesy Tecta

Tendo
Armchair
Designed by Fumio Okura, 1993.
Front legs, arms, and back of continuous piece of curved white ash
plywood, steel rod back legs, seat with upholstered cushion.
H 31-1/8", W 22", D 19-5/8"
Courtesy Tendo

Tendo
Armchair
Designed by Toshimitsu Sasaki, 1990.
Curved plywood back and arm, continuing to one leg, two legs
of tubular steel, seat with upholstered cushion.
H 27-5/8", W 21-1/2", D 25-5/8"
Courtesy Tendo

Driade (available through Luminaire)
Fina Filipina
Designed by Oscar Tusquets.
Stackable armchair with metal structure, aluminum back legs, shell of colored rattan.
Seat H 25-1/2", W 25-3/4", D 32-3/4"
Courtesy Luminaire

Thonet
Cava Chair
Designed by Studio Arrben, c. 1990.
Oval tubular steel frame, leather seat and back.
H 28-1/2", W 22-1/2", D 21-1/2"
Courtesy Thonet

Driade (available through Luminaire)
Boom Rang
Designed in 1991.
Stackable chair with frame of stiff polyurethane with steel inserts.
H 31-1/8", W 24", D 19-1/4"
Courtesy Luminaire

Driade (available through Luminaire)
Costes
Designed by Philippe Starck, c. 1982.
Frame of tubular steel painted black, shell in curved plywood, seat of foam cushion covered in black leather.
H 31-1/2", W 18-3/4", D 21-1/2"
Courtesy Luminaire

Driade (available through Luminaire)
Pratfall
Designed by Philippe Starck, c. 1982.
Tub chair with tubular steel frame painted black, curved plywood shell, cushion seat with black leather.
H 33-3/4", W 24", D 30-3/8"
Courtesy Luminaire

75

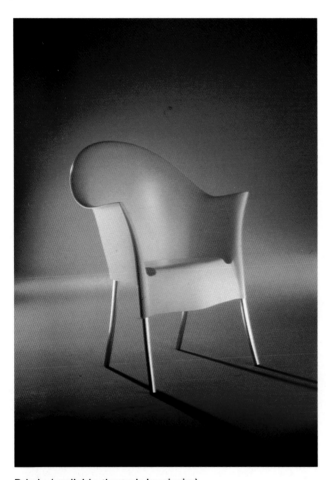

Driade (available through Luminaire)
Lord Yo
Designed by Philippe Starck, c. 1992.
Stackable armchair of polypropylene on aluminum
structure, suitable for outdoors.
H 37-1/4", W 25", D 26"
Courtesy Luminaire

Cassina
Dakota
Designed by Paolo Rizzatto.
Dining/conference chair with four-leg base supporting
shell covered in saddle leather or fabric.
H 31", W 22", D 20-1/2"
Courtesy Cassina

ICF
Vico Collection
Chair shell of four-part laminated, molded cherry or maple
veneered, or ebonized; chrome-plated steel tube legs;
removable foam seat or seat and back cushions, uphol-
stered to specification; stacks 5 high.
H 30-3/4", W 25-1/4", D 22"
Courtesy ICF

Knoll (Studio)
Diamond Chair
Designed by Harry Bertoia, 1952.
Frame of welded steel rods in polished or satin chrome
or bonded rilsan; upholstered seat cushion or fully
upholstered versions available.
H 30", W 33-1/2", D 28-1/2"
Courtesy Knoll

Knoll (Studio)
Bertoia Collection
Designed by Harry Bertoia, 1952.
Large Diamond Chair, Diamond Chair, Bird High Back Chair and Ottoman,
Side Chairs, and Barstool; produced continuously by Knoll.
Courtesy Knoll

Knoll
Womb Chair
Designed by Eero Saarinen, 1947.
Tubular steel base, fiberglass-reinforced
plastic shell, latex foam padding and
loose seat and back cushions, covered in
fabric.
H 35", W 39-3/8", D 35-1/2"
Courtesy Knoll

ICF
Swan Chair (with Egg Lounge Chair)
Designed by Arne Jacobsen, 1958.
Sculptural chair with steel-reinforced,
injection-molded, foam-covered shell
upholstered to
specification;
polished
aluminum X-
base with
glides; invisible
tilt mechanism
and swivel
base.
H 29-1/4", W 29-
1/4", D 26-3/4"
Courtesy ICF

Vitra (also available through Luminaire)
Eames Chaise
Designed by Charles and Ray Eames,
1948.
Although the prototype was entered in
a design competition sponsored by the
Museum of Modern Art in 1948, it was
not produced until 1990, by Vitra. Also
called "La Chaise," intended as a
punning homage to the sculptor
Gaston Lachaise, it consists of two thin
molded fiberglass shells cemented
together on a base of chrome-finished
steel rods and natural oak.
H 35-1/2", W 53", D 34"
Courtesy Luminaire

ICF
Egg Lounge Chair
Designed by Arne Jacobsen, 1958.
Sculptural lounge chair with steel-
reinforced, injection-molded, foam-
covered shell upholstered to specification; polished aluminum X-base with
glides, available with matching
ottoman; invisible tilt mechanism and
swivel base.
H 42", W 34", D 31"
Courtesy ICF

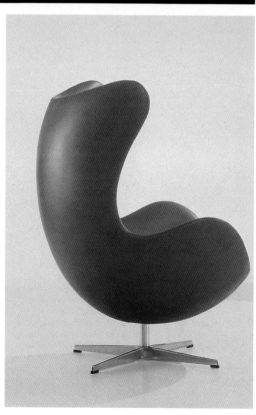

78

Artifort
584-585-592
Designed by Geoffrey Harcourt.
Chairs on swivel metal pedestal base, pressed beechwood shell, upholstered with molded foam covered in fabric.
H 37-3/8" or 38-5/8", W 33", 35-3/4", or 38-5/8", D 33-7/8", 34-5/8", or 38-5/8"
Courtesy Artifort

79

Knoll (Studio)
Tulip Arm Chair
Designed by Eero Saarinen, 1957.
Base of rilsan-coated cast aluminum; shell of molded
fiberglass-reinforced plastic; removable foam cushion
upholstery.
H 32", W 26", D 23-1/4"
Courtesy Knoll

Cassina
Dakota
Designed by Paolo Rizzatto.
Dining/conference chair with single pedestal base supporting shell
covered in saddle leather or fabric.
H 31", W 22", D 20-1/2"
Courtesy Cassina

ICF
Caribe Chair
Designed by Ilmari Tapiovaara.
Graceful swivel seat of foam-covered steel,
upholstered to specification, on oxidized
bronze-plated hob-nailed base.
H 32", W 20", D 23"
Courtesy ICF

80

Knoll (Studio)
Platner Side Chairs (with Table)
Designed by Warren Platner, 1966.
Frame forms of vertical steel wire rods welded to circular horizontal and edge-framing rods; upholstered foam cushions attached to molded fiberglass shell; also available in larger Lounge Chair.
H 28-3/4", W 26-1/2", D 22"
Courtesy Knoll

Thonet
Club Tub
Designed by Thonet design staff, c. 1972.
Adaptation of Anton Lorenz's 1930 design, this version with altered dimensions and enclosed back; 1" diameter 13 gauge tubular steel frame, upholstered seatback.
H 29-1/2", W 27", D 25"
Courtesy Thonet

Cassina
Friedman Armchair with Stool
Designed by Frank Lloyd Wright, 1956.
Wright designed the armchair with footstool for the Allen Friedman house in Bannockburn, Illinois in 1956. It was based on two earlier designs, a prototype for the Kaufmann store offices in 1935 and another version for Wright's son David in 1951. Wright also had three made for his office at Taliesen.
H 28-1/2", W 28-7/8", D 27-1/2"; footstool H 15-1/2", W 23-1/4", D 23-1/4"
Courtesy Cassina

Design America
Rohde Lounge Chair
Designed by Gilbert Rohde c. 1930s.
Tub back upholstered chair with overstuffed seat and tubular metal arm fronts and base.
H 30", W 29", D 32-1/2"
Courtesy Design America

Thonet
No. 1298 Lounge Chair
Designed by Bruno Weill, c. 1947.
Popular for institutional use in 1950s; oak face, maple core veneer frame, innerspring seat construction with upholstered seat/back.
H 31", W 28", D 30"
Courtesy Thonet

Design America
Santa Barbara
Design attributed to Kem Weber c. 1930s.
Loose cushion chair and ottoman with bent wood frames.
Chair H 35", W 29-1/2", D 37"; ottoman H15", W 24", D 30"
Courtesy Design America

Herman Miller (Herman Miller for the Home)
Eames Lounge Chair & Ottoman
Designed by Charles and Ray Eames, 1956.
Seven-ply cherry veneer shell with black leather upholstery or walnut veneer shell with sienna brown leather upholstery; 6-inch-thick urethane foam cushions; swivel mechanism in chair; die cast aluminum back braces, base and ottoman base painted black with bright polished aluminum trim; neoprene shock mounts; adjustable stainless steel glides with rubber bases.
H 32-3/4", W 32-3/4"; ottoman H 17-1/4", W 21-1/2"
Courtesy Herman Miller

Cassina
Torso Armchair
Designed by Paolo Deganello, c. 1982.
Armchair with steel structure, polyurethane foam and polyester padding upholstered in fabric or leather, seat and back may be of different fabrics.
H 45-5/8", W 43", D 35-1/2"
Courtesy Cassina

Arc Age
Doble Arm Chair
Designed by Behshad
Shokouhi, c. 1994.
Curved steel back legs and
exposed frame support,
straight front legs, uphol-
stered arms, seat, and back,
with leopard print fabric.
H 32", W 29", D 31"
Courtesy Arc Age

Arc Age
Del Arm Chair
Designed by Behshad
Shokouhi, c. 1994.
X-shape steel legs and
exposed frame support,
upholstered arms, seat,
and back with rounded
camel-like form.
H 38", W 36", D 30"
Courtesy Arc Age

Arc Age
Zaman Arm Chair
Designed by Behshad
Shokouhi, c. 1994.
Curved steel legs and
exposed frame support,
upholstered arms, seat, and
back with rounded form.
H 36", W 36", D 30"
Courtesy Arc Age

Arc Age
Pasha Arm Chair
Designed by Behshad
Shokouhi, c. 1994.
Completely curvilinear
design with curved steel
legs and exposed frame
support, stuffed uphol-
stered cylindrical arms,
upholstered seat/back.
H 36", W 38", D 30"
Courtesy Arc Age

Thonet
Bentwood Club Chair
Designed by J & J Kohn design staff, c. 1902.
Original Viennese avant-garde design with upholstered interior and wood veneer exterior;
adaptation fully upholstered with sinuous spring seat interior.
H 31", W 26-1/2", D 26"
Courtesy Thonet

Brayton (Steelcase Design Partnership)
Ergo
Designed by Damir Perisic.
Lounge and dining chairs with curved side/back base leaving open space under the
seat; hardwood frame, upholstered with polyurethane foam and polyester fiber
covered in leather or fabric.
H 28-1/2" to 32", W 26" to 29-1/2", D 26-1/2" to 28-1/2"
Courtesy Steelcase

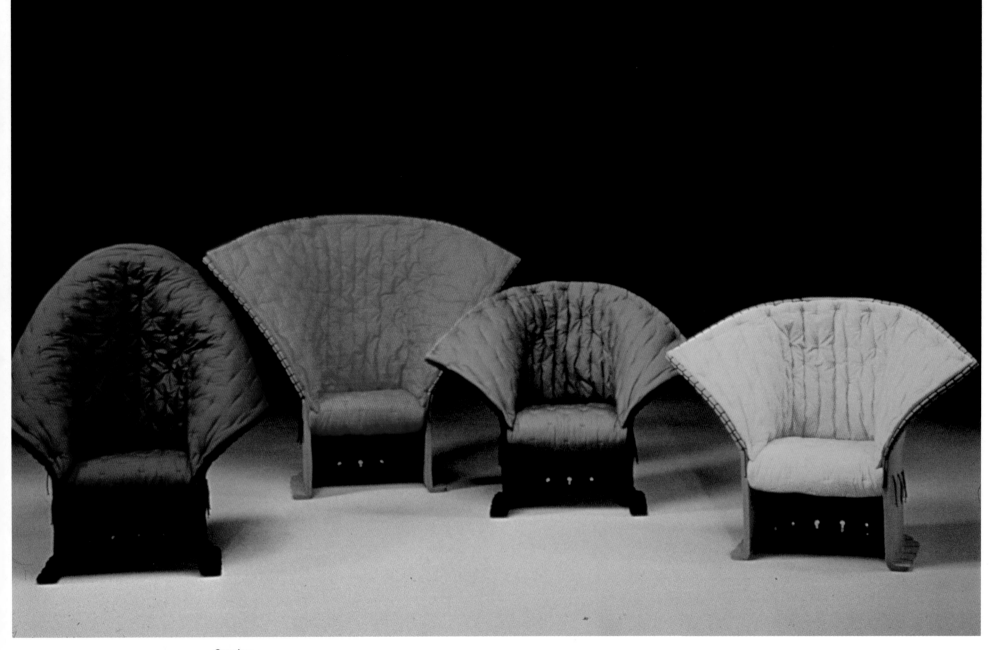

Cassina
Feltri
Designed by Gaetano Pesce.
High armchair and low armchair made of thick wool felt; the seat fixed to the supporting frame with hempen
strings; available in various colors of quilted fabric.
H 38-1/2" or 51-1/4", W 28-3/4", D 26"
Courtesy Cassina

87

Cassina
Feltri High Armchair
Designed by Gaetano Pesce.
H 51-1/4", W 28-3/4", D 26"
Courtesy Cassina

Cassina
Palmaria
Designed by Vico Magistretti.
Armchair with tubular steel frame; flexible backrest; single
cushion seat, back, and arms; removable upholstery in
fabric or leather.
H 36-1/2", W 40-1/2", D 35-3/4"
Courtesy Cassina

ICF
Ronda Armchair
Designed by Afra and Tobia Scarpa, 1986.
Fully upholstered lounge chair in fabric or leather, over
molded polyurethane foam on steel and fiberglass frame.
H 32", W 38-1/2", D 29"
Courtesy ICF

88

Artifort
Ben Chair
Designed by Pierre Paulin.
Upholstered armchair with continuous
design, the sides extending to the floor with
aluminum sledge base and open space
under the flat seat.
H 29-1/2", W 28", D 30-3/4"
Courtesy Artifort

Montis (available through Luminaire)
Loge
Designed by Gerard Van Den Berg, c.
1989.
Upholstered armchair with aluminum feet,
with ottoman.
Chair H 31-1/2", W 29-1/2", D 42-1/2";
ottoman H 14-1/4", L 23-3/4", W 19-3/4"
Courtesy Luminaire

Kron
Lauro Lounge Chair
Designed by Jorge Pensi.
Comfortable lounge seating collection to
complement the Lauro office chairs;
hardwood frame, seat and back
cushions of varying densities, arm caps
of bent plywood, black ABS legs.
H 30", W 28", D 30"
Courtesy Kron

B&B Italia (available through
Luminaire)
Florence
Designed by Antonio Citterio.
Armchair on high aluminum legs,
available in two seat depths, the
deeper with optional metallic mesh
footrest that retracts under the seat.
H 36-1/4", W 29-1/2", D 33-1/2" or
38-1/2"
Courtesy Luminaire

89

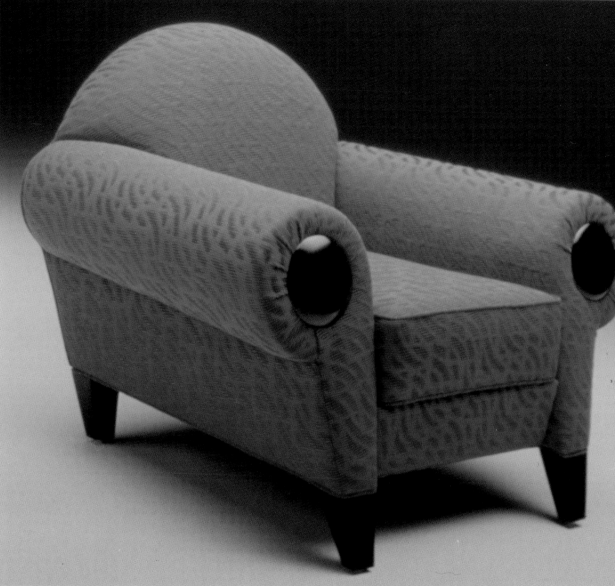

Design America
Hudson Hornet Chair
Designed by Luis Henriquez c. 1990.
Upholstered armchair with short wooden legs, cylindrical arm with disc detail in wood or covered in leather or textile.
H 30", W 41", D 38"
Courtesy Design America

Palazzetti
Armchair
Designed by Jean Michel Frank, c. 1930s.
Solid hardwood covered in polyurethane foam; cushions of
foam and down; wood feet; based on a model used by Frank
in the interiors designed for Madame Cerf.
H 37", W 32-5/8", D 31-1/2"
Courtesy Palazzetti

ICF
Hans Koller Armchair
Designed by Josef Hoffmann, 1911.
From the Koller Lounge Seating Collection: seat and
back foam-covered hardwood frame with rubber
webbed springing; upholstered to specification with
piped or welted edges.
H 37", W 35-1/2", D 32"
Courtesy ICF

Brueton Industries
Melrose Chair
Designed by Stanley Jay Friedman, 1992.
Upholstered tub shape chair with curved back lowering to
the arms, thick seat, and wood legs.
H 29", W 30", D 42"
Courtesy Brueton

Opposite page:
Top left: Design America
Aragon Dining/Lounge Chair
Designed by Martin Linder c. 1990.
Upholstered in fabric or Spinneybeck leather, legs in wood or leather-covered.
H 32" W 23" or 26", D 26" or 28"
Courtesy Design America

Bottom left: ICF
Villa Gallia Armchair
Designed by Josef Hoffmann, 1913.
From the Villa Gallia Seating Collection: seat and back foam-covered hardwood frame with
rubber webbed springing, upholstered to specification with piped edges; legs of ebonized
wood.
H 30-3/4", W 31", D 28-1/2"
Courtesy ICF

Kron
Flavia
Designed by José Luis Pérez Ortega.
Graceful lounge seating collection featuring curved lines,
raised seat back, molded tight seat cushions, and softly
sculpted wood legs.
H 33", W 30", D 29"
Courtesy Kron

Thonet
Rasen Chair
Designed by Thonet design staff, c. 1990.
Lounge seating with tapered front leg and diminished rear
leg; fully upholstered.
H 27", W 27", D 26-1/2"
Courtesy Thonet

Artifort
Mushroom Chair
Designed by Pierre Paulin, 1960s.
Tubular steel frame with horizontal springing, upholstered
with fabric over molded foam.
H 26-3/8", W 35-3/8", D 33-1/2"
Courtesy Artifort

Top left: Design America
Tucker Chair
Designed by Michael Wolk c. 1990.
Sculptural overstuffed chair with wood finish legs and a cartoonish character.
H 28", W 38", D 33"
Courtesy Design America

Top right: Design America
Swingtime
Designed by Michael Wolk c.1990.
Armchair with leather upholstery and tapered wood legs.
H 33", W 29, D 31-1/2"
Courtesy Design America

Bottom left: Brueton Industries
Champagne Chair
Designed by Victor J. Dziekiewicz, 1992.
Upholstered lounge chair shaped like an opening flower or a baseball glove, with eight sections, on round metal feet; named "champagne" because it was called the "bubble chair" during production.
H 33", W 34", D 36"
Courtesy Brueton

Brueton Industries
Sophia Chair
Designed by Stanley Jay Friedman, 1996.
Dramatic lounge chair with wing-like arms flaring outwards at back level; large loose pillow, contrasting colors.
H 42", W 56", D 42"
Courtesy Brueton

Design America
Zephyr Chair
Designed by Dan Friedlander and Ken Gilliam c. 1990.
Overstuffed chair, upholstered in fabric or Spinneybeck leather, legs in wood or leather-covered.
H 35-1/2", W 41-3/4" D 41-3/4"
Courtesy Design America

Opposite page:
Top left: Design America
Mayfair
Designed by Martin Linder c. 1990.
Sculptural upholstered side chair with only seat and back forms.
H 33", W 21", D 32"
Courtesy Design America

Top right: Brueton Industries
Morpheus Chair
Designed by Stanley Jay Friedman, 1993.
Upholstered armless chair with scroll back in contrasting colors, thick seat cushion, and tubular metal legs.
H 28", W 22", D 28"
Courtesy Brueton

Bottom left: Design America
Riverside Drive Chairs (with Rialto Cabinet)
Designed by Martin Linder c. 1990.
Armchairs with seat extending to the floor, upholstered in fabric or Spinneybeck leather.
H 29-1/2", W 26", D 32"
Courtesy Design America

Bottom right: Brueton Industries
Polo Chair
Designed by Stanley Jay Friedman, 1994.
Exaggerated box-like design with low arms, large seat extending to the floor, contrasting welting.
H 28", W 32", D 31-1/2"
Courtesy Brueton

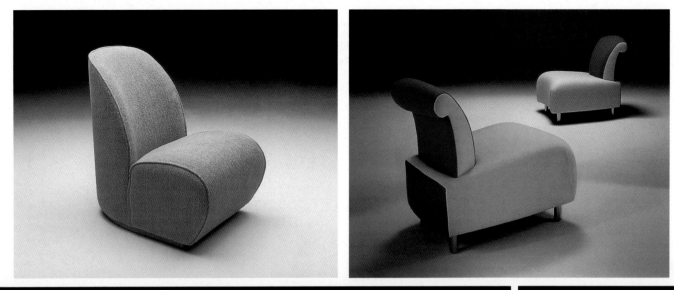

96

Opposite page:

Top left: Design America
Sutton Place Chair
Designed by Martin
Linder c 1990.
Upholstered lounge
chair with plinth base
wrapped in leather.
H 34", W 34", D 39"
*Courtesy Design
America*

Top right: Design
America
America Chair
Designed by Martin
Linder c. 1990.
Sculptural lounge chair,
seat extending to plinth
base wrapped in leather;
Little and Middle
America Chairs available
with swivel base.
H 35 -1/2", W 39",
D 40-1/2"
*Courtesy Design
America*

Bottom left: Design
America
**New York, New York
Chair**
Designed by Luis
Henriquez c. 1990.
Lounge chair uphol-
stered in fabric or
Spinneybeck leather,
curved arms with arm
trays in wood, granite,
or marble.
H 30", W 32", D 36"
*Courtesy Design
America*

Bottom right: Design
America
Spinnaker Chair
Designed by Tom
Deacon c. 1990.
Lounge chair with
exaggerated sides and
oversized seat cushion,
with steel plate feet in
polished or satin finish
or in black.
H 31-1/2" W 32", D 31"
*Courtesy Design
America*

Top left: Design America
Broadway Ltd. Chair
Designed by Martin Linder c. 1990.
Sculptural lounge chair of only four elements; Spinneybeck leather or fabric upholstery,
contrasting welting.
H 33-1/2", W 38", D 38"
Courtesy Design America

Bottom left: Design America
Flight Chair
Designed by Paul T. Frankl c. 1930s.
Upholstered armchair with exaggerated streamlined arms and two-tiered back cushion.
H 30", W 35-1/2", D 41"
Courtesy Design America

Top right: Cassina
Utrecht Armchair
Designed by Gerrit T. Rietveld, 1935.
Upholstered lounge chair in geometric design, with open arms in L-shape, contrasting
welting emphasizes the lines.
H 27-1/2", W 25-1/2", D 33-1/2"
Courtesy Cassina

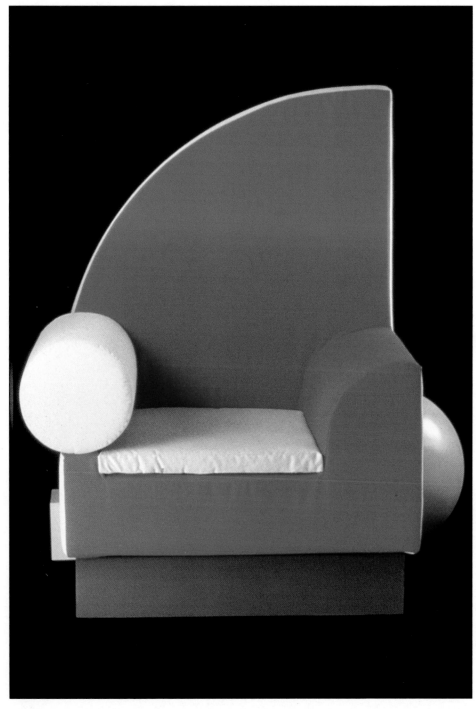

98

Opposite page:
Left: Memphis
Bel Air
Designed by Peter Shire,
1982.
Asymmetrical armchair in
wood with wool or cotton
upholstery, with dramatic
back of quarter-circle form
and cylindrical arm.
H 49-1/4", W 45-1/4", D 43-
1/4"
Courtesy Memphis

Right: Kron
Manolete
Designed by Alberto
Lievore.
Dramatic asymmetrical
design named after the late
Spanish toreador, echoes
the line of the bullfighter's
hat and red cape draped
over the arm; available in
one-arm, two-arm, armless,
and a settee.
H 50", W 24", D 26"
Courtesy Kron

Right: Artifort
Tongue Chair
Designed by Pierre Paulin, 1967.
Single continuous sculptural form of
tubular steel frame with horizontal
springing, upholstered with fabric on
molded foam.
H 25-1/4", W 33-1/2", D 35-1/2"
Courtesy Artifort

Bottom left: Artifort
F 598
Designed by Pierre Paulin, c. 1973.
Sculptural ribbon-like upholstered
chair with curved seat flowing into
supporting sides.
H 24-3/4", W 33-1/2", D 26-3/4"
Courtesy Artifort

Bottom right: Artifort
Ribbon Chair
Designed by Pierre Paulin, 1966.
Sculptural ribbon form seat with
matching ottoman, on high fre-
quency pressed wooden base.
H 29-1/8", W 39-3/8", D 29-1/8"
Courtesy Artifort

Above: Vitra
Grandpa Chair
Designed by Frank O. Gehry, 1987.
Chair of multi-layers of bonded
corrugated cardboard, with sides
and back resembling a cape.
H 36-1/2", W 46-1/2" D 48", seat H.
16-1/4"
Photo Hans Hansen, Courtesy Vitra

Top right: Vitra
Little Beaver
Designed by Frank O. Gehry,
1980/87.
Sculptural lounge chair and footstool
of multi-layers of bonded corrugated
cardboard.
Chair H 34-1/4", W 32", D 34";
Footstool H 16-1/4", W 17-1/2", D22"
Courtesy Vitra

Opposite page:
Top left: Design America
Avalon Arm Chair & Ottoman
Designed by Luis Henriquez c. 1990.
Lounge chair and ottoman in geometric block-like
design, upholstered in fabric or Spinneybeck
leather.
H 26-3/4", W 33", D 34-1/2"
Courtesy Design America

Top right: Tendo
Kashiwado Chair
Designed by Isamu Kenmochi, 1961.
Built of blocks of Japanese cedar, forming a U-
shape profile with the wood grains arranged in a
decorative pattern. The stout appearance inspired
the name Kashiwado, a famous sumo wrestler.
H 24-3/4", W 33-1/2", D 30-1/4"
Courtesy Tendo

Bottom left: ICF
Kubus Seating
Designed by Josef Hoffmann, 1910.
Armchair and 2-seat Sofa with grid design uphol-
stery in Vienna Modern style; hardwood frame,
rubber webbed springing, foam padding covered
in leather to specification; legs of black wood cubes
with hemispherical feet.
H 28-1/2", W 36" or 65", D 30-1/2"
Courtesy ICF

Bottom right: ICF
Palais Stoclet Chair
Designed by Josef Hoffmann, 1911.
Chair with continuous line from arms to curved
back; solid hardwood frame, foam covered
upholstery to specification, with covered nailheads;
legs of ebonized wood.
H 31-1/2", W 35-1/2", D 33-1/2"
Courtesy ICF

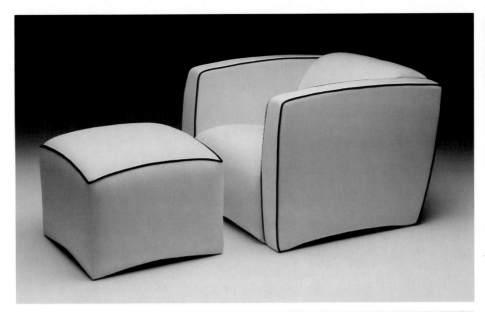

Vitra (also available through Luminaire)
How High the Moon
Designed by Shiro Kuramata, 1987.
Sculptural chair has volume without mass, of nickel-plated expanded metal.
H 29-1/2", W 37-1/2", D 33-1/2"
Courtesy Vitra

Thonet
Articula
Designed by Dewey Hodgon, c. 1990.
Tubular steel legs, maple molded plywood support and arm rest, foam cushion upholstery; contrasting colors emphasize the form.
H 32", W 33-3/4", D 27-1/2"
Courtesy Thonet

Arc Age
El Señor Arm Chair
Designed by Behshad
Shokouhi, c. 1994.
Upholstered armchair
with added seat
cushion, supported by
steel frame and short
steel legs.
H 36", W 50", D 40"
Courtesy Arc Age

Cassina
LC2 (Grand Comfort)
Designed by Le Corbusier,
Pierre Jeanneret, and Charlotte
Perriand, 1925/1928.
Armchair with tubular steel
frame in a variety of finishes;
fabric or leather upholstered
cushions.
H 26-3/8", W 30", D 27-1/2"
Courtesy Cassina

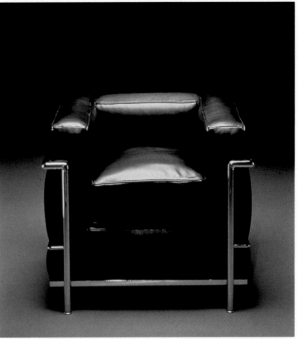

Arc Age
Fut Arm Chair
Designed by Behshad
Shokouhi, c. 1994.
Straight steel legs and
exposed frame
support, upholstered
arms, seat, and back
comprised of blocks,
with loose seat
cushion.
Courtesy Arc Age

Memphis
Roma
Designed by Marco Zanini,
1986.
Armchair in fiberglass with
iridescent finish, of solid
geometric form, without legs.
H 35-1/2", W 39-3/4",
D 35-1/2"
Courtesy Memphis

103

2: Lounges, Sofas, & Beds

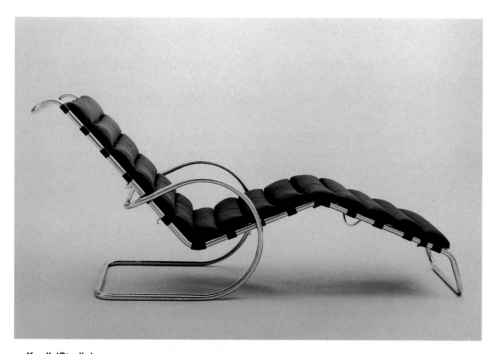

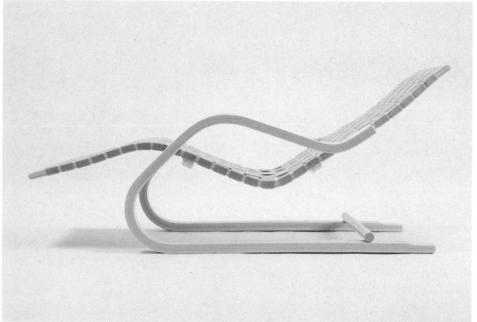

Knoll (Studio)
Mies van der Rohe MR Lounge
Designed by Ludwig Mies van der Rohe, 1929.
Tubular stainless steel frame; upholstery of cowhide belting straps crafted in a series of
quilted and seamed cushion sections.
H 31-3/4", W 25-1/2", L 70-1/4"
Courtesy Knoll

ICF
Aalto Chaise Lounge
Designed by Alvar Aalto, 1936.
Cantilevered frame of laminated bent natural birch, with seat and back in webbing or
quilted leather.
H 26", W 25-1/2", D 63-1/2"
Courtesy ICF

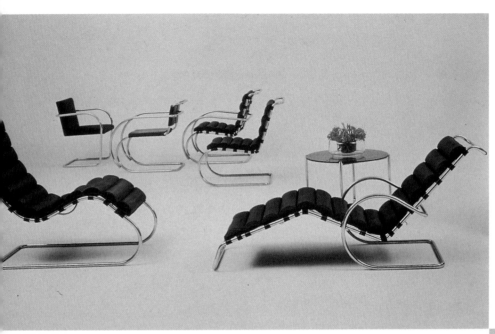

Knoll (Studio)
Mies van der Rohe MR Collection
Left, armless Lounge Chair; right, Lounge
Chair with Arms; center, Arm Chairs.
Courtesy Knoll

Knoll (Studio)
Mies van der Rohe Collection
Designed by Mies van der Rohe, c. 1929.
(left) Barcelona Lounge Chair, made almost
entirely by hand; stainless steel frame, foam
seat and back cushions covered in leather
with button tufting.
H 30", W 30", D 30"
(top right) Couch, the first piece by Mies to
combine wood and metal.
H 15-1/2", W 78", D 39"
Courtesy Knoll

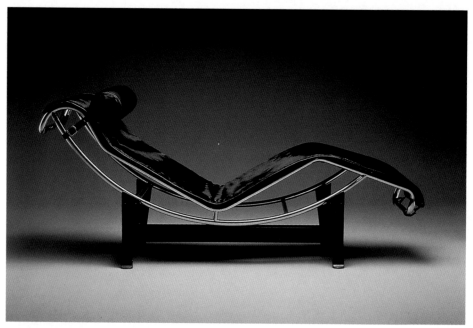

Top left: Cassina
LC4 Chaise Lounge
Designed by Le Corbusier, Pierre Jeanneret, and Charlotte Perriand 1925/1928.
Chaise lounge with adjustable chromed or matte black cradle, matte black base, upholstered in pony skin, with black leather headrest.
L 63", W 22-1/4"
Courtesy Cassina

Top right: Cassina
LC4 Chaise Lounge
Designed by Le Corbusier, Pierre Jeanneret, and Charlotte Perriand, 1925/1928.
Chaise lounge with adjustable chromed or matte black cradle, matte black base, upholstered in black leather.
L 63", W 22-1/4"
Courtesy Cassina

Bottom left: Herman Miller (Herman Miller for the Home)
Eames Chaise Lounge
Designed by Charles and Ray Eames in 1968.
Aluminum frame coated in eggplant-color nylon, black leather upholstery
L 76-1/2", W 18"
Courtesy Herman Miller

Cassina
Wink
Designed by Toshiyuki Kita, c. 1980.
Armchair that transforms into a lounge by adjusting the back and folding out the base; steel construction, fabric or leather upholstery over foam.
H 15" to 40-1/8", L 35-1/2" to 78-3/4", W 32-5/8"
Courtesy Cassina

Alias (available through Luminaire)
Longframe
Designed by Alberto Meda, c. 1993.
Chaise lounge of extruded aluminum profile and die-cast aluminum elements with polyester net seat.
H 35-1/2", W 21-1/4", L 57-1/2"
Courtesy Luminaire

108

Tecta
D52 Bench/Settee
Designed by Walter Gropius, 1911.
Settee with angular wood ash frame, open arms, finished in white or black; upholstered
seat and back with flat cushion.
H 31", W 55-1/8", D 22"
Courtesy Tecta

Design America
Knickerbocker Settee
Designed by Gilbert Rohde, early 1930s.
Settee with open wood arms and upholstered tight seat.
H 32", W 45", D 23"
Courtesy Design America

Opposite page:
Left: Thonet
Café Daum Settee
Designed by Michael Thonet, c. 1850.
Elaborate scrolling back detail of this settee indicative of the fashionable Rococo Revival style popular in Vienna
during the mid-nineteenth century. Bentwood was the only medium able to achieve such intricacy; steambent
beechwood frame, natural splined cane seat.
H 38 1/2", W 57 1/2", D 22"
Courtesy Thonet

Right: Thonet
Shades Settee (with chair)
Designed by Studio Diemme Architectural Design, c. 1990.
Settee resembles a pair of sunglasses from the front; beechwood steambent frame, upholstered foam padded seat
and back.
H 28-1/2", W 41-1/2", D 23-1/2"
Courtesy Thonet

ICF
White Settee (with Table and Chair)
Designed by Eliel Saarinen, c. 1910.
Hand-carved in Finnish Jugendstil style, the frame of solid birch lacquered pearl white.
H 26-5/8", W 35-1/4", D 27-1/2"
Courtesy ICF

Design America
Cassino Settee (with Club Chair)
Designed by Luis Henriquez c. 1990.
Legs available in wood or leather-covered; upholstered in fabric or Spinneybeck leather.
Chair H 30", W 28-1/2", D 30"; Settee H 30", W 73-1/2", D 30"
Courtesy Design America

Opposite page:
ICF
Blue Settee
Designed by Eliel Saarinen, 1929.
Art Deco inspired design with frame of solid birch, lacquered gray-blue with gold painted
detail, seat upholstered in blue jacquard designed by Irma Kukkasjarvi, or to specification.
H 30", W 48-3/4" to 114-5/8", D 21-3/4"
Courtesy ICF

Artifort
Orbit
Designed by Wolfgang C. R. Mezger.
Comfortable 3-seater with straight back in the form of waves, aluminum legs and optional arms of circular form, metal frame covered with molded foam and upholstery in contrasting colors.
H 31-1/2", W 70-7/8" or 83-7/8", D 32-1/4"
Courtesy Artifort

Vitra
Area
Designed by Antonio Citterio and Oliver Löw.
Two or three-seat sofa with continuous backrest; frame of cast aluminum with chrome finish; seat upholstered foam on wood frame; shown with add-on armrests.
H 31-1/2", W 56-1/2" or 87-1/2", D 26-3/4"
Courtesy Vitra

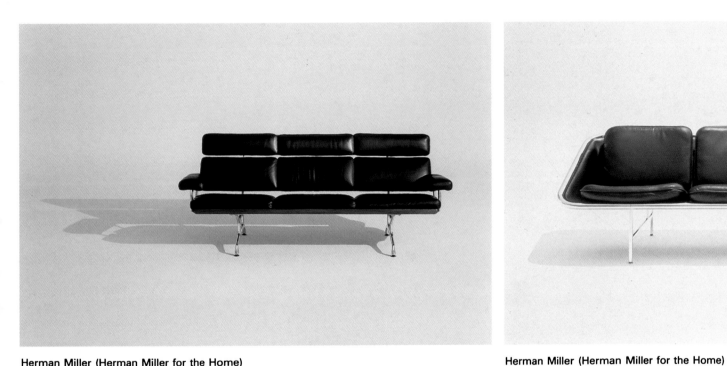

Herman Miller (Herman Miller for the Home)
Eames 3-Seat Sofa (Soft Pad)
Designed by Charles and Ray Eames in 1984.
Walnut frame and back, polished aluminum legs and arm supports, black leather upholstery.
H 33", W 80", D 30"
Photo Phil Schaftsma; courtesy Herman Miller

Herman Miller (Herman Miller for the Home)
Nelson Sling Sofa
Designed by George Nelson, 1964.
Black leather upholstery; urethane foam cushions; brightly polished chrome-plated tubular steel frame and base; neoprene and reinforced rubber webbing support slings; stainless steel adjustable glides, cushioned in rubber.
H 29-3/4", W 87", D 32-1/4"
Photo Phil Schaftsma; courtesy Herman Miller

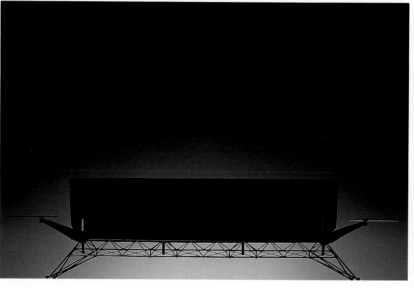

Kron
Waldorf
Designed by Jorge Pensi.
Collection of loveseat, two and three-seat sofas: hardwood frame seat cushions of down-feather/dacron blend wrapped around foam, back and arm cushions down-feather/dacron blend, cushion covers removable, beechwood legs finished black; individual backrests mechanically adjustable.
H 30-35", W 69", D 36"
Courtesy Kron

Top right: DePadova (available through Luminaire)
Safran
Designed by Vico Magistretti.
Sofa arrangement for maximum variety by combining elements of different sizes and colors.
H 31-1/2", largest L 100-3/8", D 33-1/2"
Courtesy Luminaire

Vitra
Wing Sofa
Designed by Roy Fleetwood, 1988.
Base of chromed welded steel wire beam; two round glass pivoting end tables attached to the frame; seat and back black leather over foam cushions, on hardwood platform.
H 31-1/2", L 88-1/2", D 29-1/2"
Courtesy Vitra

114

B&B Italia (available through Luminaire)
Happyhour
Designed by Andreas Störiko.
Sofa with each section able to recline independently; matte brushed aluminum and stainless steel frame.
Sofa H 36-1/4" to 44-1/8", L 71-2/3" or 100-13/16", D 36-1/4"
Footrest DM 27-9/16", H 18-1/8"
Courtesy Luminaire

Arc Age
El Señor Love Seat
Designed by Behshad Shokouhi, c. 1994.
Curved steel exposed frame, supporting fully upholstered two-seat love seat, in choice of fabrics.
H 36", W 74", D 40"
Courtesy Arc Age

Cassina
LC2 Grand Comfort
Designed by Le Corbusier, Pierre Jeanneret, and Charlotte Perriand, 1925/1928.
Sofa with tubular steel frame in a variety of finishes; fabric or leather upholstered cushions.
H 26-3/8", W 51-1/4", D 27-1/2"
Courtesy Cassina

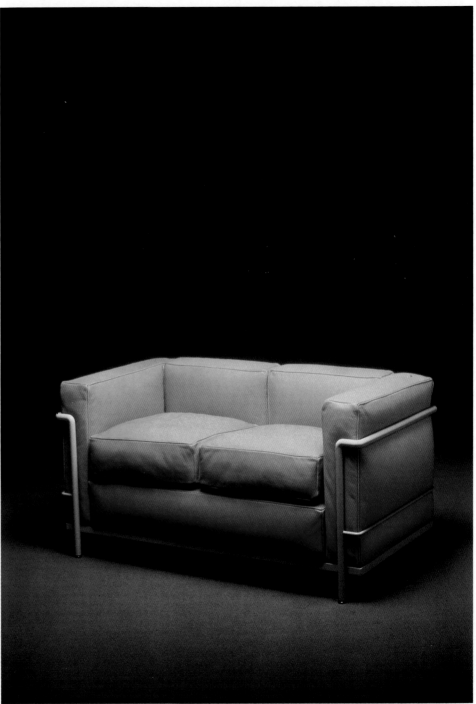

115

ICF
Ronda Two-Seat Sofa
Designed by Afra and Tobia Scarpa, 1986.
Fully upholstered lounge chair in fabric or leather, over molded polyurethane foam on steel and fiberglass frame.
H 32″, W 65-1/2″, D 29″
Courtesy ICF

Memphis
Lido
Designed by Michele De Lucchi in 1982.
Couch in wood, plastic laminate, and metal, upholstered in wool or cotton.
H 35-1/2″, W 59″, D 37-1/2″
Courtesy Memphis

116

Cassina
Robie 3 Sofa
Designed by Frank Lloyd Wright, 1908.
Two-seat sofa with cantilever tables for arms was made for the Robie house in Chicago in 1908. Reissue of cherry or beech veneer frame.
H 29-7/8″, L 94″, seat H 16-7/8″, arm H 25″.
Courtesy Cassina

Artifort
Piazza
Designed by Wolfgang C. R. Mezger.
Sofa in 1, 2, or 3 seat size, with wooden frame upholstered in molded foam; back of foam over metal frame, arms of black coated metal or black stained ash, arm cover stained ash or pear wood, optional tabletops attached.
H 31-1/2″, W 72-1/2″ plus 9-1/2″ to 23-5/8″, D 30-3/4″
Courtesy Artifort

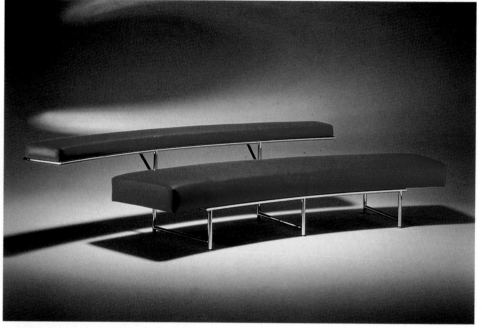

Memphis
Dublin
Designed by Marco Zanini, 1981.
Couch in plastic laminate, metal, and nonflammable synthetic fabric, appears to be propped up on a table.
H 31-1/2", W 72-3/4", D 30"
Courtesy Memphis

ClassiCon (available through Luminaire)
Monte Carlo
Designed by Eileen Gray in 1929.
Unique sofa design with soft curve and separate backrest of upholstered cushion on metal frame.
H 15-3/4" and 23-5/8", L 110", D 37-3/8"
Courtesy Luminaire

Artifort
Orbit
Designed by Wolfgang C. R. Mezger.
Comfortable 3-seater with curved back in the form of waves, aluminum legs
and arms of circular form, metal frame covered with molded foam and
upholstery in contrasting colors.
H 31-1/2", W 80" or 84", D 33-1/2"
Courtesy Artifort

Cassina
Torso Sofa
Designed by Paolo Deganello, c. 1982.
Sofa with steel structure, polyurethane foam and polyester padding upholstered in
fabric or leather, seat and back may be of different fabrics; optional table fixed to
one end.
H 45-5/8", W 57", D 35-1/2"
Courtesy Cassina

Montis (available through Luminaire)
Cabinet
Designed by Ulf Moritz, 1991.
Asymmetrical settee with ornate curve of the back, pressed stainless steel feet.
H 30-1/4" L 80-3/4", D 35-1/2"
Courtesy Luminaire

Cassina
Utrecht Sofa
Designed by Gerrit T. Rietveld, 1935.
Curved back and seat, with L-shaped arms and contrasting welting, like matching Armchair.
H 40", W 80-1/4"
Courtesy Cassina

Opposite page:
Palazzetti
Sofa & Ottoman
Designed by Isamu Noguchi, 1946.
Prototype originally made by Herman Miller; reproduction authorized by the Noguchi Foundation, of plywood on steel structure, covered in polyurethane foam; legs of natural beech, removable fabric covering.
Sofa H 30-1/4", L 98-3/8", D 46-3/4"; Ottoman H 19", W 52-1/4", D 30"
Courtesy Palazzetti

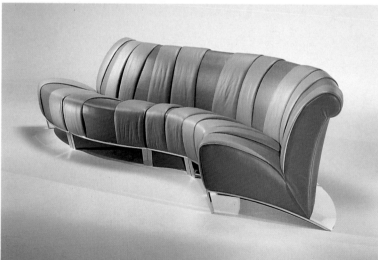

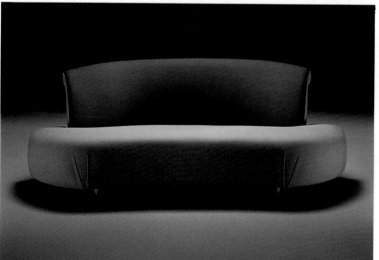

Brueton Industries
Curvee Sofa
Designed by Victor J. Dziekiewicz, 1994.
Serpentine sofa comprised of inner curve, outer curve, and straight module; metal base and legs, upholstery in contrasting alternating stripes.
Courtesy Brueton

Brueton Industries
Morpheus Sofa
Designed by Stanley Jay Friedman, 1993.
Sofa with continuous curved seat and back in contrasting colors, metal legs.
H 28", W 49", D 28"
Courtesy Brueton

Herman Miller
Chadwick Modular Seating
In apartment setting.
Courtesy Herman Miller

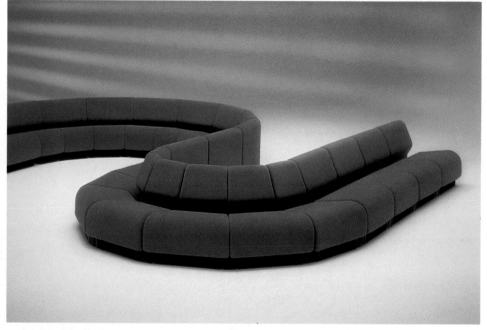

Herman Miller
Chadwick Modular Seating
Designed by Don Chadwick, 1974.
Fully upholstered molded foam modules with black molded base; modules link together in any curved or straight combination with two connectors.
H 27", widest end W 27-28", D 30"
Courtesy Herman Miller

Thonet
Robert Bernard Lounge System
Designed by Robert Aronowitz & Bernard Katzanek, c.
1978.
Foam-filled upholstered seat and back, laminated
fiberboard interior frame, wood plinth base, connectors
attach units in any configuration.
H 16-1/4" backless or 28" sections; W variable, D 31"
Courtesy Thonet

Knoll (Studio)
Pfister Lounge System
Designed by Charles Pfister, 1971.
Modular system with center, end, and corner modules for flexible configurations: frame of hard-
wood seat and back; upholstery of foam core with polyester fiber wrap or goose feathers/down,
covered in leather or fabric.
H 26" 27-1/4" to 33", D 33"
Courtesy Knoll

Bottom left: Cassina
Met Series
Designed by Piero
Lissoni & S. Sook Kim.
Three sizes of sofas,
corner units, end units,
center units, and
armchairs; steel frames,
polished aluminum
bases, polyurethane
foam cushions with
removable covers.
H 29-1/2", W 49-1/4", D
33-1/2"
Courtesy Cassina

Bottom right: Cassina
Met Series
Designed by Piero
Lissoni & S. Sook Kim.
Three sizes of sofas,
corner units, end units,
center units, and
armchairs; steel frames,
polished aluminum
bases, polyurethane
foam cushions with
removable covers.
H 29-1/2", W 71" or
98", D 33-1/2"
Courtesy Cassina

Cassina
Fiandra
Designed by Vico Magistretti.
Modular seating units with wooden structure,
polyurethane foam and polyester padding,
detachable covers in fabric or leather.
H 28-3/4", W 29" to 46", D 37"
Courtesy Cassina

Cassina
Met Series
Designed by Piero Lissoni & S. Sook Kim.
Three sizes of sofas, corner units, end units, center units, and armchairs; steel
frames, polished aluminum bases, polyurethane foam cushions with removable
covers; square, rectangular, and round occasional and coffee tables with plastic
laminate, wood, or aluminum tops.
Courtesy Cassina

B&B Italia (available through Luminaire)
Charles
Designed by Antonio Citterio.
Sofa and adjustable system of seats comprised of fourteen pieces; single wide cushion, independent back cushions, aluminum feet.
H 27-1/2", L 37-3/8" to 89-3/4", D 28-3/8"
Courtesy Luminaire

Brueton Industries
Polo Sofa
Designed by Stanley Jay Friedman, 1994.
Two or three-seat sofa with deep seat extending to the floor, low arms, contrasting welting.
H 28", W 66" or 82", D 31-1/2"
Courtesy Brueton

Bottom left: Design America
Flight Sofa
Designed by Paul T. Frankl c. 1930s.
Upholstered sofa with exaggerated streamlined arms, plinth base wrapped in leather.
H 30", W 79-1/2", D 41"
Courtesy Design America

Bottom right: Design America
Westwind Loveseat
Designed by Suzanne Martinson c. 1990.
Loveseat upholstered in fabric or Spinneybeck leather.
H 28-1/2", L 49-1/4", D 39"
Courtesy Design America

Tecta
F 53 Sofa
Designed by
Walter Gropius,
1920.
Sofa of geometric
design, with
rectangular seat,
arms extending
from the back with
space between the
arm and seat;
hardwood and
steel frame, foam
cushions covered
in fabric or leather.
H 27-1/8", W
68-7/8", D 27-1/8"
Courtesy Tecta

Brueton Industries
Sophia Sofa
Designed by Stanley Jay Friedman, 1996.
Dramatic 2, 3, or 4-seat sofa with wing-like arms flaring outwards at back level; large loose
pillows, contrasting colors.
H 42", W 77-1/2", 101-1/2", or 125-1/2", D 42"
Courtesy Brueton

Design America
China Clipper Love Seat
Designed by Martin G. Lopez.
Love seat with streamlined oversized arms with three parallel lines.
H 33-1/2", W 36", D 42-1/2"
Courtesy Design America

Kron
Multipla
Designed by Jane Dillon and Peter Wheeler, c. 1991.
Sculptural modular seating system used in a variety of configurations or as free standing units, available with or
without arms or with modular armrests between units.
H 30", W 29", D 30"
Courtesy Kron

Design America
Zephyr Love Seat
Designed by Dan Friedlander and Ken Gilliam c. 1990.
Overstuffed sofa with scalloped back, upholstered in fabric or Spinneybeck leather
H 35-1/4″, W 64-1/2″ D 41-3/4″
Courtesy Design America

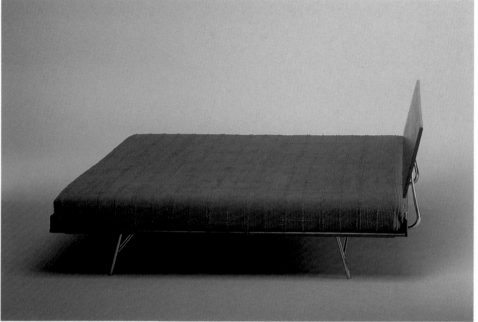

ClassiCon (available through Luminaire)
Day Bed
Designed by Eileen Gray in 1925.
Considered one of the most famous Gray designs, can be viewed from any angle.
H 24", L 74-3/4", W 33-7/8"
Courtesy Luminaire

Palazzetti
Bed
Designed by George Nelson, 1952.
Originally from the Herman Miller thin-edge series of the 1950s; reproduction of light and graceful structure in natural cherry with beechwood stave and chrome-plated base.
L 83-3/4", W 69-1/4"
Courtesy Palazzetti

Cassina (also available through Luminaire)
Xen
Designed by Hannes Wettstein.
Bed with headboard of single wood element; various pieces such as night tables or shelves
can be attached for flexibility.
H 32", L 89", W 73"
Courtesy Luminaire

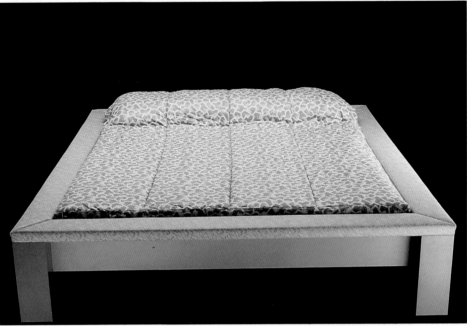

Memphis
Chelsea
Double bed in plastic laminate with padded edges and quilted bedspread (cotton fabric by
Nathalie du Pasquier); without head or foot board.
D 17-3/4", L 90-1/2", W 78-3/4"
Courtesy Memphis

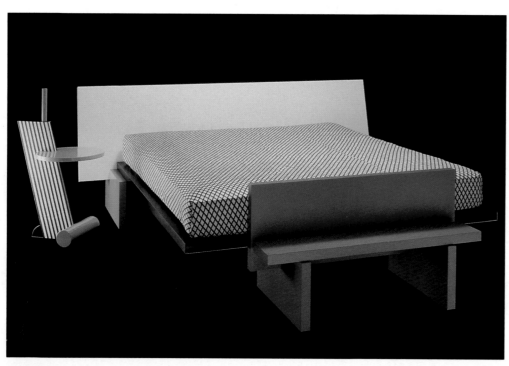

Memphis
Horizon
Designed by Michele De Lucchi, 1984.
Double bed with rectangular head and foot boards, in plastic laminate (with optional cotton bedspread by Ettore Sottsass)
H 31-1/2″, L 98-1/2″, W 86-1/2″
Courtesy Memphis

Brueton Industries
Bed Maximus
Designed by Stanley Jay Friedman, 1993.
King, queen, or double bed with wood case construction head and foot board; concealed hinge at headboard for storage compartment; continuous wrapped leather frame; 3″ channel quilted bedding.
Courtesy Brueton

Design America
Ocean Drive Bed
Designed by Luis Henriquez c. 1990.
Platform bed available in standard, queen, and king sizes
Queen H 51", L 104", W 69"
Courtesy Design America

B&B Italia (available through Luminaire)
Aletto
Designed by Paolo Piva.
Headboard of cotton mesh stretched over aluminum frame
H 39-3/8", W 70-3/4", 75", or 78-3/4", L 89" or 93"
Courtesy Luminaire

3: Benches & Stools

Shaker Workshops
Meetinghouse Bench
The Shakers used light, portable benches in their meetinghouses, like this example made at the Enfield, New Hampshire community c. 1840.
H 31 1/2", W 50"
Courtesy Shaker Workshops

Herman Miller
(Herman Miller for the Home)
Nelson Platform Bench
Designed by George Nelson in 1946 (produced until 1967, reintroduced 1994). Solid maple in ebonized or clear and ebonized finish.
H 14", W 18-1/2", L 48" or 60"
Photo Phil Schaftsma; courtesy Herman Miller

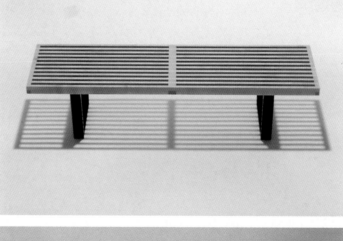

Tendo
Bench
Designed by Riki Watanabe, 1960. Long bench made of pine, for use in public places, echoes the curving roofs of Shinto architecture.
H 15-1/2", W 69-3/4", D 17-3/4"
Courtesy Tendo

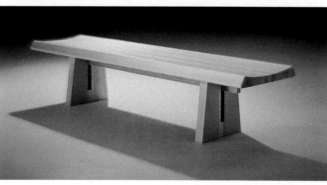

Tendo
Bench
Long bench with dark finish wood base and contrasting light colored rippled molded plywood top, giving the effect of waves.
H 17", W 78-3/4", D 19-5/8"
Courtesy Tendo

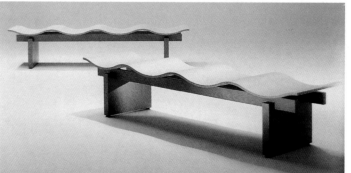

Tendo
Butterfly Stool
Designed by Sori Yanagi, 1956.
Stool with exuberant curves of
Japanese architecture, resembling a
butterfly; two molded plywood shells
connected with metal rods, can be
assembled at home.
H 15-11/16", W 16-9/16", D 12-3/16"
Courtesy Tendo

Tendo
Stool
Designed by Reiko (Murai) Tanabe,
1960.
Made of three identical panels of
molded plywood glued together;
can be used as a seat or table.
H 14-3/16", W 17-11/16",
D 17-11/16"
Courtesy Tendo

Herman Miller
Eames Walnut Stool (three designs)
Designed by Charles and Ray Eames, 1960.
Solid walnut finished in gunstock oil; concave top and bottom surfaces; available in three shapes.
H 15", top DM 13-1/4"
Courtesy Herman Miller

135

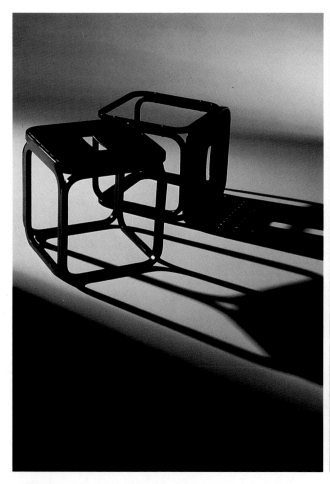

Thonet
Austrian Postal Savings Bank Stool
Designed by Otto Wagner, c. 1906.
Steambent beechwood leg and seat frames with aluminum
cap detailing; veneer molded plywood seats with
perforated design and hand hold; adaptation of original
Thonet design by Wagner.
H 18-1/2", 16-1/4" square
Courtesy Thonet

Thonet
Bentwood Stools
Designed by Michael Thonet, c. 1866.
In 1866 Thonet issued their second catalog, displaying
seventy items. Stools were among the new designs and,
for the first time, the leg brace was added to all but the
luxury models, to improve stability; steambent wood
frames, wood saddle seat.
H 18" or 30"; W 17", D 17", seat DM 14"
Courtesy Thonet

ICF
Aalto Stools
Designed by Alvar Aalto, 1930-1933.
Legs of natural birch, tops natural or stained birch veneer,
linoleum, or white plastic laminate.
H 17-1/4" or 25-5/8", DM 13-3/4", 15", or 19"
Courtesy ICF

136

Thonet
Breuer Stools
Designed by Marcel Breuer, c. 1933.
Breuer employed tubular steel in a
cantilever design as a stool, and it is still
used extensively; each with elastic strap
seat bases and foam in upholstered seats.
Fitting Stool of 14 gauge tubular steel
frame, Barstool of 11 gauge tubular steel
frame.
Fitting H 18", W 16-1/2", D 17-1/2"; Barstool
H 28", W 18", D 19-1/2", Footrest H 10"
Courtesy Thonet

ICF
Spaghetti Stools
Designed by Giandomenico Belotti, c. 1982.
Chromed or baked epoxy finish steel frame; seat and back in colored spaghetti-like strips of PVC.
H 18", W 17-3/4", D 15-3/4"
Courtesy ICF

137

Knoll (Studio)
Risom Stool
Designed by Jens
Risom, 1941.
Select clear maple
hardwood in clear
finish, mortise and
tenon construction,
upholstery of 2-inch
straps of cotton
webbing.
H 17-1/8", W 16-1/2",
D 15-1/8"
Courtesy Knoll

Vitra
W.W. Stool
Designed by Philippe
Starck, 1991.
One-piece high stool,
originally designed for
director Wim Wenders,
produced in a limited
series; sand-blasted,
cast aluminum with
green finish.
H 38", W 22", D 21"
Courtesy Vitra

Arc Age
Moft Bar Stool
Designed by
Behshad Shokouhi, c.
1994.
Gently splayed steel
legs, available in
three finishes,
upholstered seat.
H 41", W 17", D 19"
Courtesy Arc Age

Arc Age
Moft Stool
Designed by Behshad
Shokouhi, c. 1994.
Two straight steel legs,
two curved, and curved
support connecting to a
single stretcher;
upholstered seat.
H 30", W 17", D 19"
Courtesy Arc Age

B&B Italia (available through Luminaire)
Arcadia
Designed by Paolo Piva, c. 1985.
Stools of light alloy and padded seat, with various backrests of structural steel wrapped in
cold-foamed polyurethane.
H 30-3/4" to 44", W 18-1/8" to 25-1/2", D 20" to 23-1/2"
Courtesy Luminaire

Thonet
Fledermaus Bar Stool
Designed by Thonet design staff, c 1984.
Adaptation of Hoffmann chair design; of steambent beechwood with
upholstered foam cushion, plywood seat interior, and brass footplate.
H 41-1/2", D 18", W 22-1/2"
Courtesy Thonet

Thonet
Sof-Tech Barstool
Designed by David Rowland, c. 1979.
Plastic-coated spring material on seat and back gives transparent effect; 7/8" diameter 14 gauge tubular steel frames with minimal parts for mass production.
H 42", W 22", D 20-1/2"
Courtesy Thonet

Brueton Industries
Tux Bar Stool
Designed by Stanley Jay Friedman, 1994.
Polished or satin tubular steel frame, leather or fabric upholstered seat and back, the back and back legs in the form of coat tails extending to the floor.
H 42", W 19", D 21"
Courtesy Brueton

Alias (available through Luminaire)
Spaghetti Stools
Designed by Giandomenico Belotti, c. 1982.
Chromed or baked epoxy finish steel frame; seat and back in colored spaghetti-like strips of PVC or leather.
H 18" to 31-1/2", W 18", D 15-3/4" or 19-3/4"
Courtesy Luminaire

Thonet
Hoffmann Barstool
Designed by Thonet design staff, c. 1960.
Adaptation of Josef Hoffmann's 1930's bentwood design, for bar and counter use; steambent wood frames, foam in upholstered versions, plywood seat interior, brass ring footrest.
H 43-1/2", W 20-1/2", D 20"
Courtesy Thonet

Arc Age
Doble Bar Stool
Designed by Behshad Shokouhi,
c. 1994.
Variation of the Moft Stool, with
backrest connected to front
stretcher by two curved pieces;
steel frame, upholstered seat/
back.
H 41", W 15", D 18"
Courtesy Arc Age

Arc Age
Shabnam Executive Bar Stool
Designed by Behshad
Shokouhi, c. 1994.
Four gently splayed steel legs,
the front with thicker portions;
upholstered seat/back.
H 31", W 19", D 18"
Courtesy Arc Age

Arc Age
El Señor Bar Stool
Designed by Behshad Shokouhi,
c. 1994.
Curved backrest attached to
continuous steel back legs, wavy
front legs; upholstered seat/back.
H 42", W 20", D 20"
Courtesy Arc Age

Arc Age
El Señor Set
Designed by Behshad
Shokouhi, c. 1994.
Stool with curved backrest
attached to continuous steel
back legs, wavy front legs;
upholstered seat/back.
H 42", W 20", D 20"
Courtesy Arc Age

141

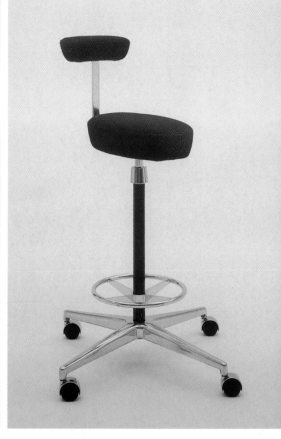

Thonet
Breuer Bar Stool
Designed by Thonet design staff.
Adaptation of 1928 Breuer design, natural cane back insert,
splined construction.
H 43-1/2", W 18-1/4", D 22-1/2"
Courtesy Thonet

ICF
Caribe Bar Stool
Designed by Ilmari Tapiovaara.
Graceful swivel seat of foam-covered steel, upholstered to
specification, on oxidized bronze-plated hob-nailed base, with
optional foot ring.
H 36", W 19", D 18", foot ring DM 16"
Courtesy ICF

Herman Miller
Perch
Designed by Robert Propst, 1964.
Originally part of Action Office 1 as an alternative
seating unit to relieve sedentary workers; suited
for home or office for temporary mobile sitting or
perching at any "stand-up" work surface; small
foam-padded seat with separate padded backrest
(also used as a leaning siderest or frontrest)
attached to chrome-finished metal spline; pedestal
base with adjustable heights, foot ring, four-star
base with casters.
max H 43", max seat H 33", W 10-5/8", D 15-1/2"
Courtesy Herman Miller

4: Tables

ClassiCon (available through Luminaire)
Occasional Table
Designed by Eileen Gray, 1927.
Light, mobile, easily adjustable table with tubular steel frame and round or square top in high gloss finish.
H 22", W 14-1/8" or 15-3/4"
Courtesy Luminaire

Cassina
Kick
Designed by Toshiyuki Kita, c. 1983.
Adjustable side table on casters, with dark gray enamel base and pneumatic gas cylinder for height adjustment; oval top in lacquered acrylic. H 15-3/4" to 20-5/8", W 19-5/8"
Courtesy Cassina

Design America
Bach Table
Designed by Alphonse Bach c. 1930s.
Table with tubular metal base and two wood shelves.
H 23", L 25-1/2", W 11"
Courtesy Design America

Thonet
Breuer Occasional Tables
Designed by Marcel Breuer, c. 1930.
These occasional tables evolved from Breuer's stool/
nesting table design. Currently of 1" diameter 14 gauge
tubular steel frame with either 1/2" smoke gray glass or
3-1/6" Thonet Plastic laminates.
H 16", 30" x 48"; or H 21", 30" x 30"
Courtesy Thonet

Thonet
Nesting Tables
Designed by Marcel Breuer, c. 1925.
Originally intended as a stool and used in Breuer's early
interiors, such as the canteen at the new Bauhaus building
designed by Walter Gropius in Dessau. Breuer may have
come up with the idea of the cantilever chair independently of Mart Stam when he turned his new stool on its
side. Original models were of bent nickeled steel and
laminated wood and manufactured after 1927, probably
by Gebrüder Thonet. Currently of 3/4" diameter 11 gauge
tubular steel frame and self edge laminate top.
W 22" to 26", D 14" to 20", H 18" to 24"
Courtesy Thonet

Brueton Industries
Queen's Table
Designed by J. Wade Beam, 1993.
Stainless steel base with silver and gold finish, square glass top.
H 21", 20" sq.
Courtesy Brueton

Brueton Industries
Tribeca Table
Designed by Stanley Jay Friedman, 1994.
Three-legged table with steel frame and triangular glass top.
H 18" or 25", sides 20-3/4"
Courtesy Brueton

Brayton (Steelcase Design Partnership)
McHugh
Designed by Tom McHugh.
Series of occasional tables of bar stock carbon steel structure with upper apron of laser cut sheet steel; chrome, pewter, or powder coated finishes; tops of glass, wood, or marble.
H 18-1/2" to 40", W 10-5/8" to 40-3/4", D 9-5/8" to 17-1/4"
Courtesy Steelcase

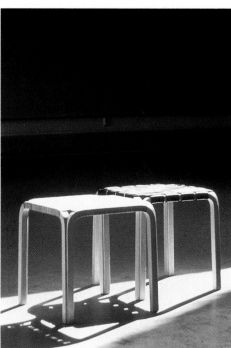

Top left: Design America
Trylon End Table
Designed by Luis Henriquez c. 1990.
Bird's-eye maple top and shelf, cherry legs (available in other material combinations).
DM 19-1/2" or 24", H 24"
Courtesy Design America

Top right: ICF
Fan-legged Table
Designed by Alvar Aalto, 1954.
Legs of natural birch, top of natural ash or mahogany veneer.
H 17-1/2" or 28", 17-3/4", 27", or 35-1/2" square.
Courtesy ICF

Bottom right: ICF
Nesting Tables
Designed by Alvar Aalto, 1933.
Classic design of three nesting tables with natural birch legs and top.
H 17-1/8" to 22-7/8", W 20" to 27-1/4", D 16-1/2"
Courtesy ICF

ICF
Hoffmann Nesting Tables
Designed by Josef Hoffmann, 1905.
Four nesting tables of solid ash with natural or ebonized finish.
H 23-5/8" to 27-1/2", W 11-1/2" to 19-3/4", D 11-7/8" to 16"
Courtesy ICF

Vitra
Easy Edges Wiggle Tables (with Side Chair)
Designed by Frank O. Gehry, 1992/72.
Approximately 50 layers of corrugated cardboard with edges finished in hardboard.
Tables H 19-1/2", 15-3/4", 20-1/2", or 24-3/4" sq.; Chair H. 32-1/4", W 14-1/4", D 24"
Courtesy Vitra

147

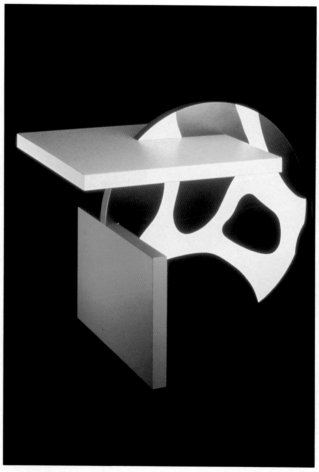

Cassina
Schroeder Table
Designed by Gerrit T. Rietveld, 1922-23.
Of black, red, and white geometric planes, creating an abstract sculptural effect.
H 23-3/4", top 20-1/4" sq.
Courtesy Cassina

Memphis
Continental
Designed by Michele De Lucchi, 1984.
Asymmetrical end table in plastic laminate of three geometric shapes placed in perpendicular arrangement.
H 27-1/2", W 35-1/2", D 23-1/2"
Courtesy Memphis

Memphis
Ivory
Designed by Ettore Sottsass, 1985.
Side table in reconstituted veneer, plastic laminate, and glass; in elongated vertical form with circular top and base.
H 39-1/2", DM 19-1/2"
Courtesy Memphis

Design America
Knickerbocker High Cafe Table (with Chair)
Designed by Luis Henriquez, c. 1990. Round table with three rings supporting the legs, like the three or four slats on chair arms; contemporary adaptation of a Gilbert Rohde design.
H 39-1/2", DM 30" or 36"; chair H 40-1/2", W 21"
Courtesy Design America

Thonet
Fledermaus Table
Designed by Josef Hoffmann, c. 1908. Using classicism for inspiration, Hoffmann introduces the imagery of a fluted column with decorative balls; steambent maple wood frame, round top, optional brass trim on base, inset top covered in vinyl or plastic laminate.
H 30" with 30", 36" or 42" DM top, and 19" or 26" DM base.
Courtesy Thonet

Knoll (Studio)
Toothpick Cactus Tables
Designed by Lawrence Laske, 1993. Occasional tables with round or oval top of wood veneer or Italian slate; base of a cluster of 6-16 tapered maple legs.
H 16" or 20", round top DM 20", 26", or 35-3/4"; oval 42" x 24" or 54" x 27"
Courtesy Knoll

149

Knoll (Studio)
Saguaro Cactus Tables
Designed by Lawrence Laske, 1993.
Side tables with 4-leg base of bent laminated hard maple or polished aluminum; top of wood veneer or Italian slate.
H 20", top DM 20" or 26"
Courtesy Knoll

Palazzetti
Table
Designed by Ernest Race, 1951.
Part of an outdoor furniture line made for the 1951 Festival of Britain; of bent steel wire covered in black or white PVC.
H 27-1/2", DM 24"
Courtesy Palazzetti

Alias (available through Luminaire)
Tree Table
Designed by Paolo Rizzatto, c. 1991.
Base of die-cast aluminum in polished or painted finish; round, oval, or palette-shaped top of wood in a variety of finishes.
H 21-5/8" to 27-1/2", DM 24", or 26-3/4" x 18-1/2"
Courtesy Luminaire

150

Driade (available through Luminaire)
Vicieuse
Designed in 1991.
Small table with frame of cast aluminum with central screw for
height adjustment; multilayered wood top with laminate finish.
H 19-5/8" to 28-3/4", top DM 15-3/4"
Courtesy Luminaire

Shaker Workshops
Rectangular Candle Stand
With arched legs dovetailed into the tapered base, top
fastened to pedestal by a rectangular cleat, of clear maple.
H 25-1/2", top 18" x 21"
Courtesy Shaker Workshops

Shaker Workshops
Harvard Side Table
Elegantly proportioned table, originally made at the
Harvard, Massachusetts community about 1840, of clear
cherry with pine drawer interior.
H 27 1/4", top 28-3/4" x 17 1/2"
Courtesy Shaker Workshops

151

Right: Herman Miller
(Herman Miller for the Home)
Nelson End Table
Designed by George Nelson,
1954.
Maple veneer edge on black
or white laminate top,
pedestal and base available
in polished aluminum or
white enamel.
H 22" & DM 17" or H 16-1/2"
& DM 28-1/2", or H 22" &
DM 28-1/2"
*Photo Earl Woods; courtesy
Herman Miller*

Below: ICF
Piet Hein Tables
Designed by Piet Hein, 1968.
Tables of various shapes and
sizes, with chromium-plated
steel legs; natural beech,
cherry, or maple wood or
plastic laminate tops.
H 27-3/4" L 31-1/2" to 118"
with extension.
Courtesy ICF

Above: Vitra (also available
through Luminaire)
Louise Table (with chairs)
Designed by Philippe
Starck, c. 1991.
Round or square-topped
table, polyester on fiber-
board top, aluminum legs,
indoor/outdoor.
H 28-1/2", DM 31-1/2" or
27-1/2" sq.
Courtesy Luminaire

Left: ICF
Caribe Table
Designed by Ilmari
Tapiovaara, 1962.
Base of oxidized bronze-
plated hobnailed one-piece
construction; top of solid
oak butcherblock or with
plastic laminate; available
in round, square, or
rectangular top.
H 28-1/2", top DM 24" to
72"
Courtesy ICF

Design America
Saturn Coffee Table
Designed by Luis Henriquez, c. 1990. Coffee table with metal base and round glass top.
DM 48″
Courtesy Design America

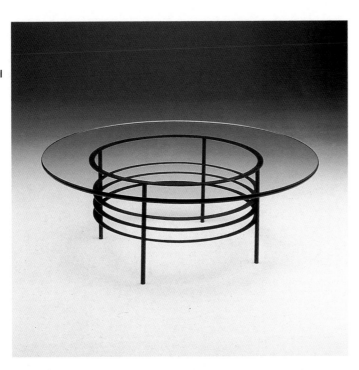

Design America
Knickerbocker Dining/Conference Table
Designed by Luis Henriquez c. 1990. Round table with three leg rings; wood or glass top.
H 29″, DM 36″, 42″, 48″, or 54″
Courtesy Design America

Cassina
Midway 3 Table
Designed by Taliesen Architects, 1914. The glass-topped dining table with steel base was created by Wright's successor firm, Taliesen Architects, Ltd. as a companion to Wright's Midway 2 Chair; reissue frame enameled in white red, or gray.
H 29″, square or round top 47-1/4″
Courtesy Cassina

Arc Age
Doble Dining Table
Designed by Behshad Shokouhi, c. 1994. Round table with slanting steel legs, curved supports, and three circular stretchers; shown with glass top.
H 29″, DM 38″
Courtesy Arc Age

153

Cassina
La Rotonda
Designed by Mario Bellini.
Round dining or conference table with base in natural ash wood, natural walnut, or stained walnut; top in clear glass or same wood finish as base.
H 29-1/8", DM 65"
Courtesy Cassina

Design America
Skylark Table
Designed by Michael Wolk, c. 1990.
Round table with stylized tripod base, in maple, cherry, or a combination.
H 29", DM 48", 54", or 60"
Courtesy Design America

Baleri Italia
President M.
Designed by Philippe Starck, c. 1982.
Demountable structure of three or four legs of steel tubing and cast aluminum, glass tops.
H 29-1/2", 53-1/2" square, or 67" x 47-1/4"
Courtesy Luminaire

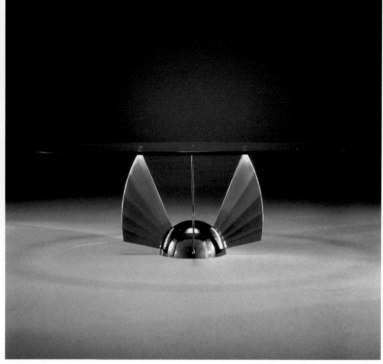

ICF
Montserrat Table
Designed by Oscar Tusquets, 1987.
Base of painted die-cast aluminum with adjustable foot levelers; top of clear glass or with etched diagonal design.
H 27-1/2"; W 51-1/4", L 51-1/4" to 98-1/2"
Courtesy ICF

Brueton Industries
Victory Table
Designed by J. Wade Beam, 1993.
Round glass top table with dramatic metal pedestal base in the form of wings extending from a half sphere to the top.
DM 36" or 42"
Courtesy Brueton

155

Top left: Cassina
LC10-P Tables
Designed by Le Corbusier, Pierre Jeanneret, & Charlotte Perriand, 1928. Square and rectangular dining and cocktail tables with polished chrome plated steel legs and enameled steel frame, with top of clear or textured glass.
H 13" or 27-1/2" W 31-1/2" to 55-1/8"
Courtesy Cassina

Top right: Alias (available through Luminaire)
Line
Designed by Alberto Meda.
Clear or matte glass top tables in square or rectangular shape; frame and legs in natural beechwood with junctions in die-cast aluminum.
35-1/2" & 55" sq. or W 35-1/2" to 47-1/4", L 63" to 94-1/2"
Courtesy Luminaire

Baker
Metal Cocktail Table
From the Savoy Collection: contemporary interpretation of French Empire styling with handcrafted reeded apron, antiqued brass saber legs, and glass or slate inset top.
H 22", W 40", D 28"
Courtesy Baker

Brueton Industries
Leggins Low Table
Designed by Victor J. Dziekiewicz, 1995.
Square or rectangular table with solid wood legs and glass top.
H 15-3/4", 36" sq. or 24 x 48"
Courtesy Brueton

156

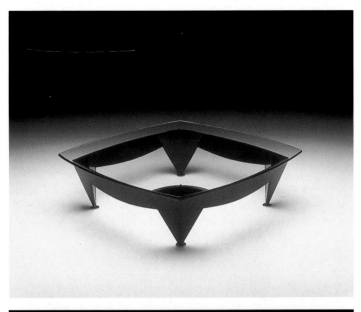

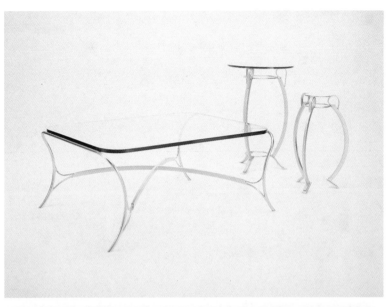

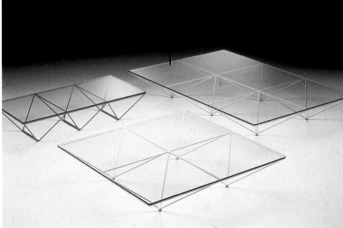

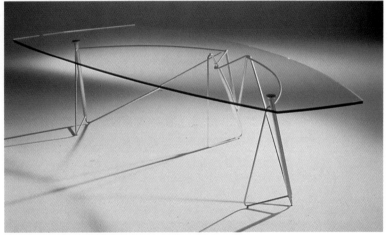

B&B Italia (available through Luminaire)
Meta
Designed by Leo Aerts & Ingrid Wijnen, c. 1987.
Coffee table made of two elements for flexible configurations -- base of lacquered

embossed wood and rotating top of hardened frosted glass.
H 19-5/8", L 59", D 23-5/8"
Courtesy Luminaire

158

Top left: Acerbis International (available through Luminaire)
Serenissimo
Designed by Lella & Massimo Vignelli, c. 1985.
Rectangular, square, or circular plane of opalescent or transparent glass over stucco-covered steel columns.
H 28-1/3", L 49-5/8" to 118-1/8", D 38-9/16" to 63"; DM 57" or 63"
Courtesy Luminaire

Bottom left: Casigliani (available through Luminaire)
Quarry
Designed by Site, 1989.
Glass top on base of black marquinia.
H 14-1/4" (without top)
Courtesy Luminaire

Top right: Casigliani (available through Luminaire)
Kono
Designed by Lella & Massimo Vignelli, 1986.
Glass top, base of white marble and red oxidized copper.
H 14-1/2", top 47" sq.
Courtesy Luminaire

Bottom right: Casigliani (available through Luminaire)
Metafora
Designed by Lella & Massimo Vignelli, 1979.
Glass top, base of beige mondragone, Roman travertine, white Carrara marble, and/or black marquinia.
H 8-5/8", top 47" sq.
Courtesy Luminaire

159

Herman Miller (Herman Miller for the Home)
Noguchi Table
Designed by Isamu Noguchi, 1948.
Originally produced by Herman Miller 1948-1973, reintroduced 1984; solid walnut base, 3/4-inch clear plate glass top.
H 15-3/4", top 50" x 30"
Courtesy Herman Miller

Memphis
Madonna
Designed by Arquitectonica, 1984.
Table in lacquered wood; kidney shape top supported on two pedestals.
H 29-1/4", L 96", W 56-3/4"
Courtesy Memphis

Opposite page:
Alivar (available through Palazzetti)
Two-part Nesting Table
Designed by Frederick Kiesler, 1935.
Biomorphic shape tables, originally designed by Kiesler for the New York apartment of fabric designer Alma Mergentine, and only one produced; reproduction of hand-finished cast aluminum.
H 9-1/2", W 37" and 23-5/8", D 25-1/4" and 16"
Courtesy Palazzetti

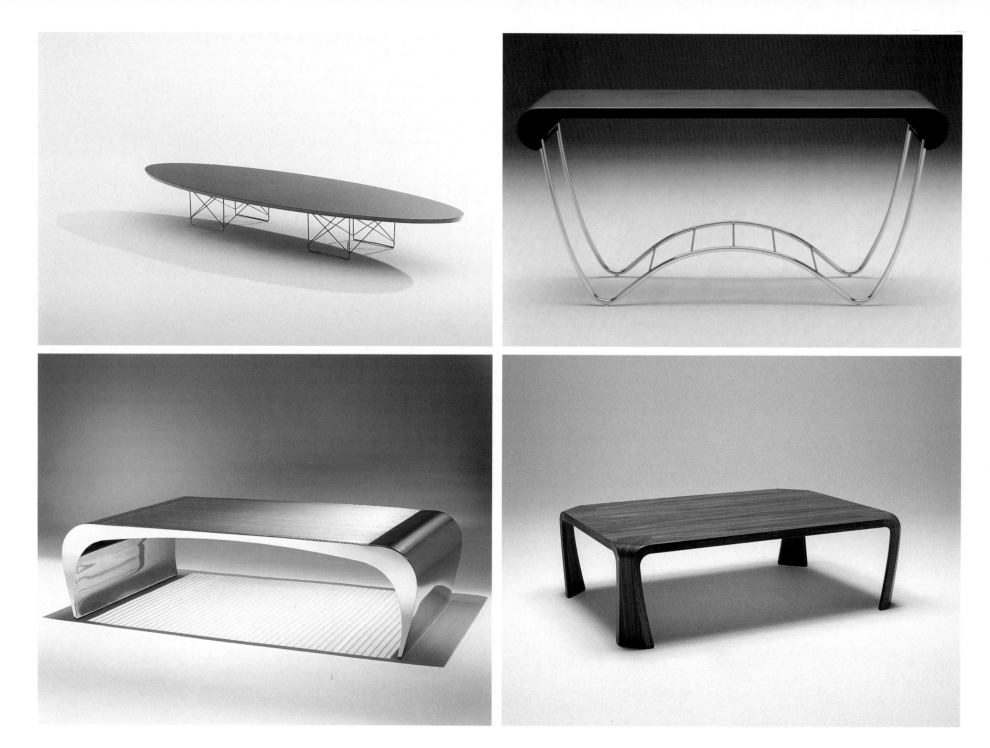

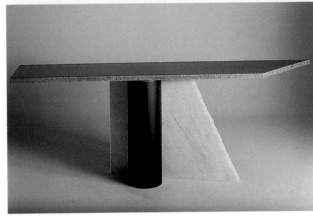

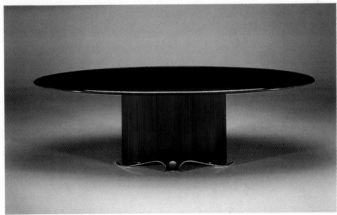

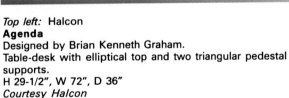

Top left: Halcon
Agenda
Designed by Brian Kenneth Graham.
Table-desk with elliptical top and two triangular pedestal supports.
H 29-1/2", W 72", D 36"
Courtesy Halcon

Bottom left: Casigliani (available through Luminaire)
Ambiquità
Designed by Lella & Massimo Vignelli, 1983.
Marble top, base of white venatino and black marquinia.
H 28-1/4", top 35-1/2" x 78-3/4"
Courtesy Luminaire

Top right: Tecta
Grande Table
Designed by Jean Prouvé, 1950.
Table with two flattened metal pedestals supporting a rectangular top of solid maple, granite or with ash veneer or linoleum.
H adjustable 28-3/4" to 29-1/2", W 89", D 33-7/8"
Courtesy Tecta

Bottom right: Brueton Industries
Virginian High Table
Designed by J. Wade Beam, 1992.
Elliptical wood drum pedestal base with metal decorative trim at the floor; 1-1/2" thick wood top.
H 29", W 84" or 96", D 42" or 48"
Courtesy Brueton

Above: **Cassina**
D.S.1 Table
Designed by Charles Rennie Mackintosh, 1918.
Table with round top and geometric grid support, ebony finish.
Courtesy Cassina

Top left: Cassina
G.S.A. Table
Designed by Charles Rennie Mackintosh, c. 1900.
Round table with center insert, legs with rectangular cutouts, two cross stretchers.
H 29", DM 74-3/4"
Courtesy Cassina

Bottom left: Cassina
G.S.A. Table
Close-up of top.
Courtesy Cassina

Top left: Knoll (Studio)
Florence Knoll Table Desk
Designed by Florence Knoll, 1961.
Oval or round table desk: frame and legs of heavy gauge welded steel; top of laminate, wood veneer or solid marble.
H 28", top DM 54"; oval 54" x 47-1/2" or 96" x 78-1/2"
Courtesy Knoll

Top right: Herman Miller (Herman Miller for the Home)
Eames LaFonda Table
Designed by Charles and Ray Eames, 1961.
Round LaFonda Table with a plastic top and double column base.
H 17-5/8", DM 30"
Courtesy Herman Miller.

Bottom right: Herman Miller (Herman Miller for the Home)
Eames Round Dining Table (Segmented Base Table)
Designed by Charles and Ray Eames, 1964.
Cherry veneer top, tubular steel columns, polished aluminum base
H 28-1/2" DM 54"
Photo Phil Schaafsma, courtesy Herman Miller.

Alias (available through Luminaire)
Atlas System
Designed by Jasper Morrison.
Table with base and pedestal support
of varying heights in steel/aluminum;
top of various shapes, of aluminum and
maple or laminate.
Courtesy Luminaire

Vecta (Steelcase Design Partnership)
Disc
Designed by William Rattery.
Series of tables with aluminum disc base, cone, and column; laminate or wood veneer top
in round, racetrack, or square shape; choice of edge treatment.
H 15", 20", or 29", DM 18" to 54"
Courtesy Steelcase

Opposite page:
Knoll (Studio)
Saarinen Collection: Tulip Dining Table, End Table, Coffee Table (with Chairs)
Designed by Eero Saarinen, 1956.
Bases of rilsan-coated cast aluminum; round or oval tops of laminate or marble.
Smallest DM 16-1/4"; largest W 96"
Courtesy Knoll

Alias (available through Luminaire)
Atlas System
Designed by Jasper Morrison.
Table system with base and pedestal
support of varying heights in steel/
aluminum; tops of various shapes, of
aluminum and maple or laminate.
Courtesy Luminaire

Herman Miller (Herman Miller for the Home)
Segmented Base Tables
Designed by Charles and Ray Eames, 1964.
Ash or cherry veneer tops, tubular steel columns, polished aluminum bases.
Courtesy Herman Miller

Top left: Herman Miller (Herman Miller for the Home)
Eames Rectangular Dining Table (Segmented Base Table)
Designed by Charles and Ray Eames, 1964.
Ash or cherry veneer top, tubular steel columns, polished aluminum base.
H 28-1/2", top 36" x 60", 36" x 72", or 42" x 72"
Photo Phil Schaafsma, courtesy Herman Miller

Bottom left: Shaker Workshops
Drop-Leaf Table
Attributed to the New Lebanon, New York community c. 1830.
Table with turned legs and double-pinned mortise-and-tenon frame, of hard maple.
H 30" W 38" with leaves up, 21-3/8" with leaves down.
Courtesy Shaker Workshops

Top right: Shaker Workshops
Serving Table
Possibly intended for the ministry's dining room, with unusual tripod foot design, of clear maple.
H 29 1/2", top 50-3/4" x 20"
Courtesy Shaker Workshops

Bottom right: Palazzetti
Shaker Drop-leaf Table
New Lebanon Community design, c. 1830.
Drop-leaf table with slender tapered legs, of cherry wood with natural finish.
H 28-3/4", W 36-1/4", D 11-3/4" to 24-3/8"
Courtesy Palazzetti

169

Top left: Cassina
D.S.1 Table
Designed by Charles Rennie Mackintosh, 1918.
Drop-leaf dining table, light finish, grid base, shown open.
H 29-1/4", top 69" x 48"
Courtesy Cassina

Bottom left: Cassina
D.S.1 Table (with D.S.3 Chairs)
Designed by Charles Rennie Mackintosh, 1918.
Drop-leaf dining table, shown with ebonized finish; rounded drop leaves extending to the floor.
H 29-1/4", top 69" x 48"
Courtesy Cassina

Top right: ICF
Aalto Multi-Section Tables
Designed by Alvar Aalto, 1933.
Originally designed as a child's table for the Viipuri Library, the adult version makes a versatile conference table. Legs of solid natural birch; semi-circular, square, or rectangular tops of birch veneer, linoleum, or plastic laminate.
H 28", DM or L 47-1/4", W 23-5/8" to 47-1/4"
Courtesy ICF

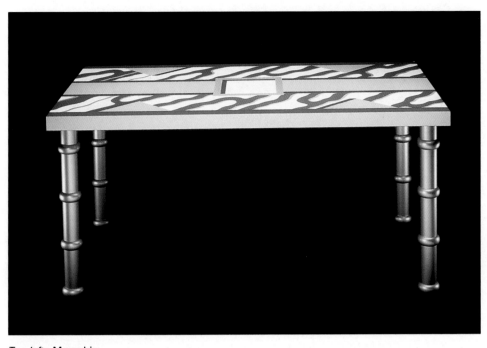

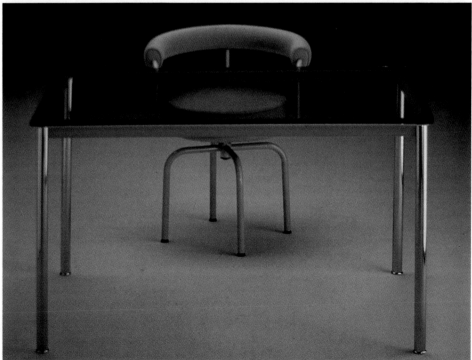

Top left: Memphis
Madras
Designed by Nathalie du Pasquier, 1986.
Table in decorated plastic laminate; top supported by four stylized bamboo-like legs.
H 29-1/2", L 63", W 33-1/2"
Courtesy Memphis

Top right: Cassina
Berlino Table
Designed by Charles Rennie Mackintosh, 1905.
Table with flat rectangular legs with vertical parallel line decoration, attached to the top at a 45-degree angle.
Courtesy Cassina

Bottom right: Cassina
LC10-P Table (with Revolving Armchair)
Designed by Le Corbusier, Pierre Jeanneret, & Charlotte Perriand, 1928.
Square and rectangular dining and cocktail tables with polished chrome plated steel legs and enameled steel frame, with top of clear or textured glass.
H 13" or 27-1/2" W 31-1/2" to 55-1/8"
Courtesy Cassina

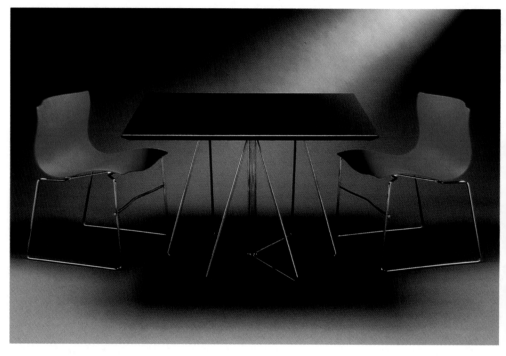

Vecta (Steelcase Design Partnership)
Ballet X-Base
Designed by Douglas Ball, c. 1989.
Table with machined aluminum inner column, cast aluminum leg section and cross bar; rectangular top in laminate or wood veneer; folding or non-folding; optional modesty panel.
H 28-1/2", various top sizes
Courtesy Steelcase

Knoll (Studio)
Paper Clip Table (with Paper Clip Chairs)
Designed by Vignelli Design, 1994.
Cafe table with base of cold rolled steel rod with fused polyester; top of 1" laminate or 1/2" clear tempered glass or 1" natural cleft slate.
H 28-1/8"; 30", 36", or 42" sq. top.
Courtesy Knoll

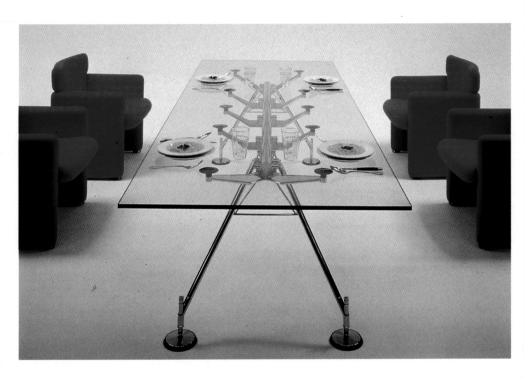

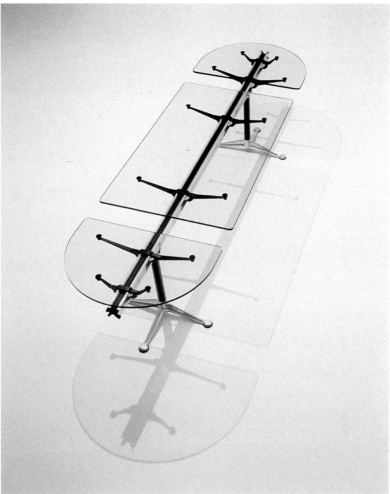

Tecno (available through Luminaire)
Nomos
Designed by Norman Foster, c. 1986.
Steel and cast aluminum base with chrome or other finish options; top of glass, supergrain, or laminate in circular, square, or rectangular shape.
H 24-1/2" or 28-1/3", seven top sizes from 47-1/4" sq. or DM, to 39-1/3" x 110-1/4"
Courtesy Luminaire

Herman Miller
Burdick Dining Table
Designed by Bruce Burdick, 1981.
Originally designed as a conference table for an executive office, it has become a popular residential dining table; rectangular top with two attached half round sections of 5/8-inch plate glass with polished edge; polished aluminum base and beam.
H 28-7/8", W 120", D 36"
Courtesy Herman Miller

173

Smith & Hawken
Salerno Rectangular Table (with Lido Chair)
Folding table allows six diners to sit comfortably and cross their legs. Heavy base supports top of commercial-grade sheet steel coated with polyester for mild weather protection.
H 29", W 47", D 30"
Courtesy Smith & Hawken

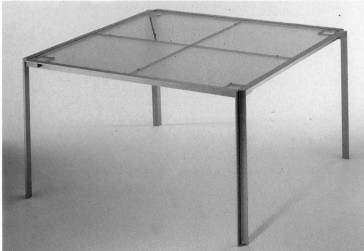

Alias (available through Luminaire)
Outdoor
Designed by Giandomenico Belotti. Table with steel frame treated with cataphoresis process, wired glass top with black rubber edge.
H 29", top 55" sq.
Courtesy Luminaire

174

Zero U.S.
Palace
Designed by Donato D'Urbino & Paolo Lomazzi.
Storage unit with American cherry or beech sidewalls, polished aluminum and cherry or beech shelves, acid etched glass doors.
H 86-5/8", W 86-5/8", D 17-3/4"
Courtesy Zero U.S.

Zero U.S.
Silvergate
Designed by Donato D'Urbino & Paolo Lomazzi.
Shelf unit configured in free-standing single or multiple units; sides of steel pipe and tube ladder coated with aluminum epoxy powder; shelves satin finished aluminum; sliding panels in translucent polycarbonate.
H 70", unit W 53-1/2", D 17-3/4"
Courtesy Zero U.S.

Zero U.S.
Abracadabra
Designed by Jonathan De Pas,
Donato D'Urbino, Paolo
Lomazzi, c. 1991.
Flexible metal bookshelf
allowing various configurations
with one or more of the glass or
aluminum shelves pressure-
mounted between floor and
ceiling or fixed to the wall.
H 79" to 138", W 24-1/2" to 54",
D 13" to 15-3/4"
Courtesy Zero U.S.

Zero U.S.
Abracadabra
Designed by Jonathan De Pas,
Donato D'Urbino, Paolo
Lomazzi, c. 1991.
Courtesy Zero U.S.

Zero U.S.
Abracadabra
Designed by Jonathan De Pas, Donato D'Urbino, Paolo Lomazzi, c. 1991.
Courtesy Zero U.S.

176

Palazzetti
Bookshelves
Designed by Marcel Breuer, c. 1930.
Chrome-plated tubular steel frame; shelves of marine plywood with high-pressure laminate;
exposed ends finished in beeswax; also available in solid ash finished in beeswax.
H 55-1/2" and 69-3/4", W 65", D 18-1/2"
Courtesy Palazzetti

Shaker Workshops
Creamery Shelves
Broad-shelved milk pan and cheese racks were used in
storage cellars and dairies, as seen in this adaptation from the
Mount Lebanon, New York community, of solid clear Eastern
white pine.
H 72", shelves W 35", D 14-1/2"
Courtesy Shaker Workshops

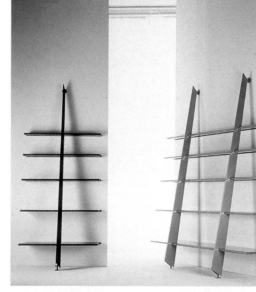

Baleri Italia (available through Luminaire)
Mac Gee
Designed by Philippe Starck, 1978.
Modular bookshelf as inclined upright to
lean against a wall, five shelves of
decreasing depth; steel with baked
epoxy finish.
H 93", W 39", D 6" to 19-3/4"
Courtesy Luminaire

Vitra
Spatio
Designed by Antonio Citterio and Glen
Oliver Löw.
Bookcase, Pedestal, and Table for office
or home workplace; natural pear wood
veneer on aluminum bases or shelf
supports.
Bookcase H 58-1/4", W 53", D 16";
Pedestal H 25-1/2", W 17-3/4", D 30-3/4";
Table H 28-1/2", L 82-1/2", W 39-1/2"
Courtesy Vitra

Cappellini (available through Luminaire)
Sistemi
System consisting of uprights, cases,
and wall panels in 31 colors, 4 wood
veneers, and a variety of finishes.
Courtesy Luminaire

Herman Miller (Herman Miller for the
Home)
Relay Credenza/Bookcase
Designed by Geoff Hollington, 1991.
Bookcase with or without glass doors
attaches to the top of credenza or
enclosed desk for storage and visual
privacy; laminate or veneer case -- full-
cut cherry or recut light ash; wire
management, adjustable shelves.
Total H 54" or 70", W 48", D 14"
Courtesy Herman Miller

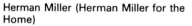

Cassina
D.S.5 Sideboard
Designed by Charles Rennie Mackintosh, 1918.
Closed cabinet on bottom, open shelves on top, of ebonized
ash wood, decorated with colored glass mosaic with lead,
inlaid with mother-of-pearl.
63-1/2" x 22-1/4" x 58-7/8"
Courtesy Cassina

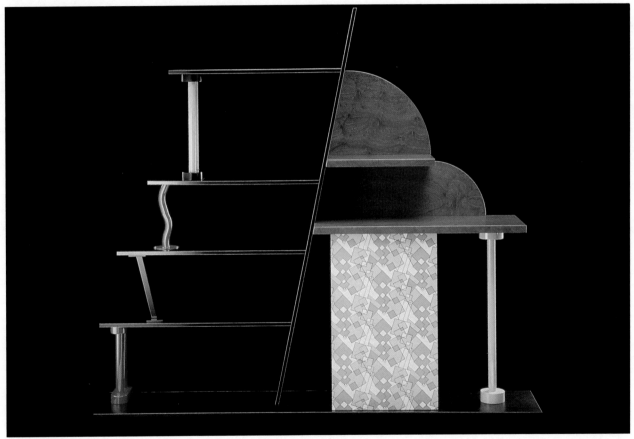

Memphis
Malabar
Designed by Ettore Sottsass, 1982.
Sideboard in plastic laminate and wood; structure in painted metal; of asymmetrical form with open side resembling
steps.
H 92-1/2", W 100"
Courtesy Memphis

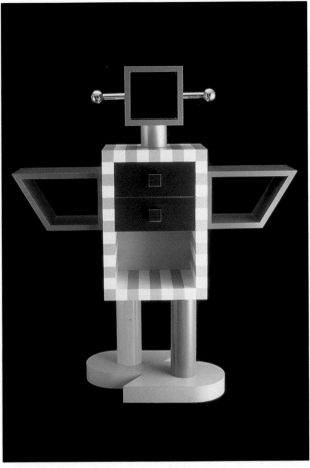

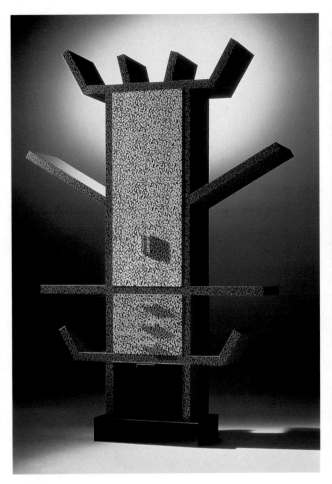

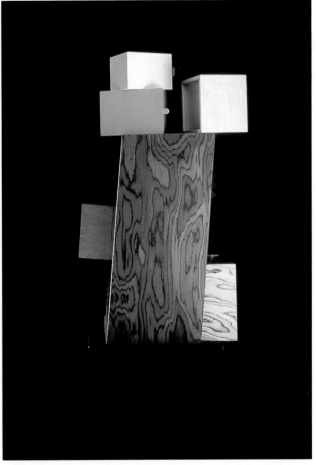

Memphis
Ginza
Designed by Masanori Umeda, 1982.
Wooden robot made of plastic laminate shelves and
drawers.
H 68-3/4", W 21-3/4"
Courtesy Memphis

Memphis
Casablanca
Designed by Ettore Sottsass, 1981.
Sideboard in plastic laminate with internal shelves and
protruding appendages in anthropomorphic gesture.
H 90", W 59-1/2"
Courtesy Memphis

Memphis
Amazon
Designed by Marco Zanini, 1985.
Cabinet in reconstituted veneer and lacquered wood;
asymmetrical form comprised of cubes attached to a
central unit.
H 80-3/4", W 38-1/2"
Courtesy Memphis

Opposite page:
Left: Memphis
Plaza
Designed by Michael Graves, 1981.
Dressing table with six drawers and stool in briar,
lacquered wood, glass, mirrors, and brass
H 92-1/2", W 60-1/4", D 20-1/4"
Courtesy Memphis

Right: Memphis
Carlton
Designed by Ettore Sottsass, 1981.
Room divider in multicolored plastic laminate; lower
drawers, levels of shelves with diagonal sides.
H 77-1/4", W 74-3/4", D 15-3/4"
Courtesy Memphis

Design America
Rialto Cabinet
Designed by
Martin Linder, c.
1990
Wood cabinet with
three drawers,
each with a
contrasting dark
band and wing-
like projection.
H 23", W 25", D
22"
*Courtesy Design
America*

Baker
Oval Cocktail Table
Designed by
Michael Vanderbyl.
From the Archetype
Collection: contem-
porary adaptation
of classic form; oval
cocktail table with
tapered legs,
drawer, of English
Sycamore veneer in
diamond motif, in
light marina finish.
H 18-1/2", W 48", D
30"
Courtesy Baker

Wogg (available
through Luminaire)
Ellipse Tower
Designed by Benny
Mosimann.
Modular units
stacked to create
towers of three
different heights;
curtain doors slide
open.
H 17-3/8" each
stackable unit; W
25-5/8", DM 19-1/2"
Courtesy Luminaire

Tecta
Container
Designed for Tecta,
1993.
Multifunctional
container with
cherry wood
interior, fine steel
exterior, drawers,
drop-front surface,
and storage
compartment for
bar items.
H 44-7/8", W
13-3/8", D 16-1/2"
Courtesy Tecta

Brueton Industries
Empire Cabinet Series
Designed by Stanley Jay Friedman.
Rectangular cabinet with Empire/Art Deco flavor; with wavy gold door handles, mounted on cylindrical metal feet.
H 80", W 60", D 24"
Courtesy Brueton

Baker
Entertainment Unit
From the Savoy Collection, the graceful ogee pediment, inlay pattern, and silver fluted footings recall a Ruhlmann sideboard design c. 1925; lacewood, laurel, and maple veneers, with silver leaf.
H 64-1/2", W 60-1/2", D 22-1/2"
Courtesy Baker

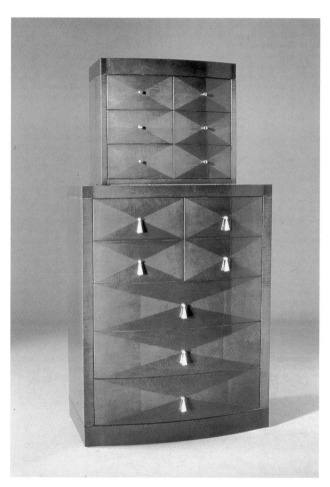

Baker
Chest on Chest
Designed by Michael Vanderbyl.
From the Archetype Collection: contemporary adaptation
of classic form; top section with six drawers and bottom
with seven, of English Sycamore veneer in diamond motif,
in presidio finish.
H 65-3/4", W 34", D 20"
Courtesy Baker

Palazzetti
Shaker Chest of Drawers
Storage pieces, both built-in and freestanding, were made in
a variety of sizes and proportion; this vertical design, c. 1805,
has six large drawers with four small drawers above; solid
cherry and veneered plywood.
H 60", W 30"
Courtesy Palazzetti

Baker
Semanier
Designed by Michael Vanderbyl.
From the Archetype Collection: contemporary adaptation
of classic form; tall, elongated chest on tapered legs,
seven drawers, of English Sycamore veneer in diamond
motif, in light marina finish.
H 72", W 24", D 20"
Courtesy Baker

184

Top left: Baker
Console
From the Savoy Collection: inspired by Emile-Jacques Ruhlmann's Art Deco designs, console of solid walnut, maple, and cherry with laurel and maple veneers and inlay.
H 32", W 57-1/2", D 20"
Courtesy Baker

Top right: Herman Miller
Relay Credenza
Designed by Geoff Hollington, 1991. Credenza with drawer, file, and cupboard combinations; laminate or veneer top and case -- full-cut cherry or recut light ash; cable management, and adjustable glides.
H 28-1/2" W 72", D 22"
Courtesy Herman Miller

Bottom left: Brueton Industries
Malaga Credenza
Designed by Stanley Jay Friedman, 1991. Art Deco style 4-door credenza with geometric design veneer, metal trim, and exaggerated tapered legs.
H 29", W 84", D 24"
Courtesy Brueton

Bottom right: Brueton Industries
Virginian Credenza
Designed by J. Wade Beam, 1992. Elliptical drum shaped credenza with Art Deco flavor; 4- or 6-door, wood case and top, metal medallion at center base.
H 29", W 72, 84, or 96", D 19"
Courtesy Brueton

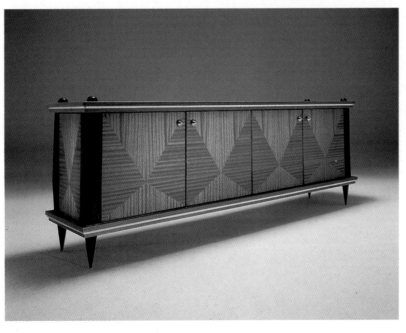

Arc Age
El Señor Credenza
Designed by Behshad Shokouhi, c. 1994.
Light mahogany credenza with mahogany top and curved steel leg supports extending up the ends of the tapered case.
H 29", W 75", D 20"
Courtesy Arc Age

Arc Age
El Señor Bar
Designed by Behshad Shokouhi, c. 1994.
Bar with curved steel leg supports extending nearly to the top of the tapered case, with vertical surfaces covered in laminate, mahogany top.
H 42", W 87", D 23"
Courtesy Arc Age

Arc Age
El Señor Bureau
Designed by Behshad Shokouhi, c. 1994.
Bureau with long curved steel leg supports extending nearly to the top of the tapered case and arched under the bottom; vertical surfaces laminate, mahogany top.
H 29", W 76", D 34"
Courtesy Arc Age

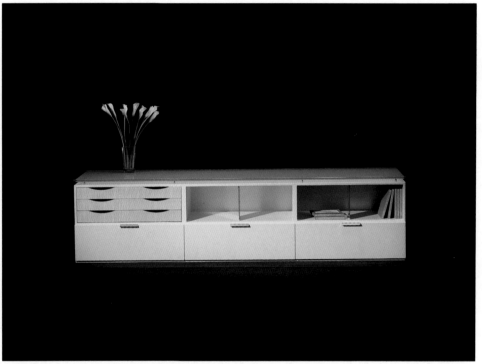

Halcon
Cadence
Designed by John Thiele and Brian Graham.
Credenza from a collection of freestanding and modular components and work surfaces; in eight natural wood veneers, eight metallic Chemcolor hues.
H 28-3/4", W 72", D 24"
Courtesy Halcon

Halcon
Attache
Designed by Lauren Rottet and Richard Riveire.
Credenza with 1/2" thick glass top; from a collection of case pieces with work surfaces; offered in a variety of woods, finishes, and colors with optional figured veneer drawers and contrasting stained edge accents.
H 29-3/4", W 108", D 24"
Courtesy Halcon

Top left: Interlübke (available through Luminaire)
Duo Bars
Designed by Peter Maly, c. 1983.
Example of one of the versatile and flexible storage systems by Interlübke; shown in room setting with other Duo storage unit and items from other companies.
Courtesy Luminaire

Top right: Interlübke (available through Luminaire)
Another Interlübke storage design, shown with items from other companies.
Courtesy Luminaire

Bottom left: Interlübke (available through Luminaire)
Storage design with items from other companies.
Courtesy Luminaire

Bottom right: Interlübke (available through Luminaire)
Medium Plus
Designed by Team Form, c. 1974.
Shown in room setting with items from other companies.
Courtesy Luminaire

Interlübke (available through Luminaire)
Storage design with items from other companies.
Courtesy Luminaire

6: Office & Public

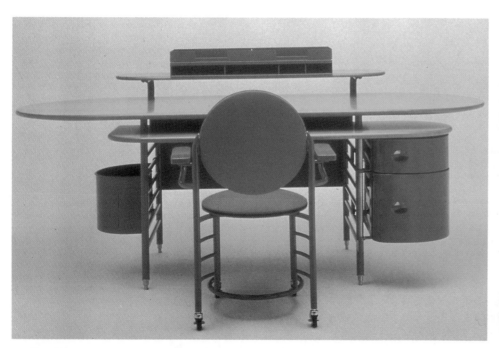

Cassina
Johnson's Wax Desk & Chair
Designed by Frank Lloyd Wright, 1937.
Painted metal and walnut desk and upholstered chair designed for the S.C. Johnson Wax Administration Building in Racine, Wisconsin in 1938, a forerunner of systems furniture; originally manufactured by Metal Office Furniture Co. (Steelcase).
Chair H 34", W 21-1/2", D 20"; Desk H 33-1/4", W 84", D 35"
Courtesy Cassina

Knoll
Albini Desk
Designed by Franco Albini, c. 1952.
Pedestal desk with frame and legs of square steel tube with chrome finish, top of polished plate glass, 2-drawer "floating" pedestal with rear open shelf.
H 27-1/2", W 48", D 26"
Courtesy Knoll

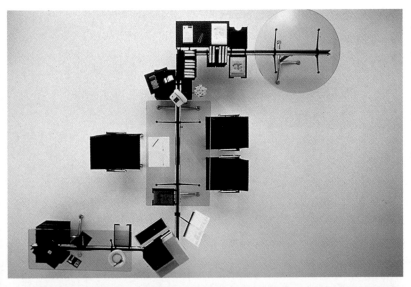

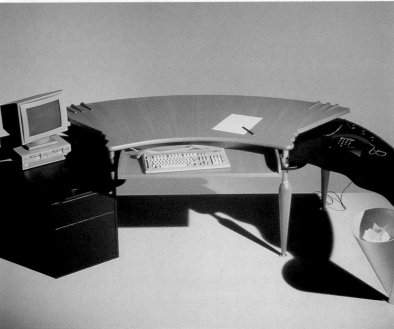

Top left: Herman Miller
Burdick Group
Designed by Bruce Burdick, 1981.
Group of tables with glass tops and aluminum bases, originally designed for executive offices, also used in residential settings; shown in one of many possible configurations.
Courtesy Herman Miller

Top right: Herman Miller
Relay
Designed by Geoff Hollington, 1991.
Collection of versatile freestanding office furniture with assortment of work surfaces and storage for a variety of options in work or home office.
Courtesy Herman Miller

Bottom left: Vitra
Sipek Office
Designed by Borek Sipek, 1992.
Worktable combination with extensions, organizer, and waste paper basket; black lacquered wood, pear veneer, metal basket.
H 29-1/2", L 118", D 59"
Courtesy Vitra

Bottom right: Vitra
Spatio
Designed by Antonio Citterio and Glen Oliver Löw.
Credenza, File, Bookcase, and Table for office or home workplace; natural pear wood veneer on aluminum bases or shelf supports.
Credenza H 24", W 63", D 23-1/2"
Courtesy Vitra

Top left: Steelcase
Personal Harbor
Self-contained private workspace provides seclusion for concentration; with ready access to surrounding collaborative spaces; easily configured, adaptable, and customized for multiple tasks; shown closed.
Courtesy Steelcase

Bottom left: Steelcase
Personal Harbor
Shown open.
Courtesy Steelcase

Top right: Steelcase
Personal Harbor
Shown clustered around common area.
Courtesy Steelcase

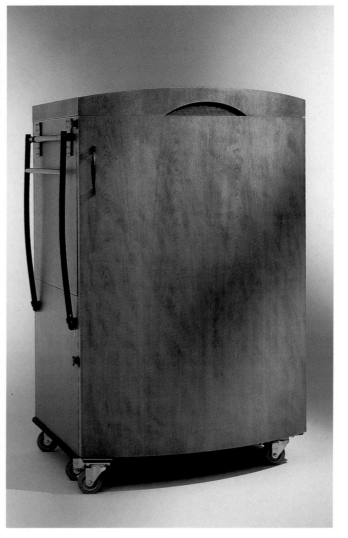

Haworth
Correspondent
Shown open
Open H 78", W 96-1/2", D 60"
Courtesy Haworth

Haworth
Correspondent
Mobile office for temporary work environment with more than
14 square feet of surface space, including a pull-out work
surface for keyboard or laptop, tackboard, marker board,
security lock, cord-drop, and air duct for heat release if
needed. Case of cherry veneer on particleboard; door cherry
veneer on formed plywood. Shown closed.
Closed H 57-1/2", W 36", D 30"
Courtesy Haworth

Top left: Haworth
Crossings
Modifiable, open-ended work station designed to give the individual working in the space control over the surroundings; components are functionally independent for improved space utilization and multi-tasking ability; shown closed.
Courtesy Haworth

Top right: Haworth
Crossings
Shown open.
Courtesy Haworth

Bottom right: Haworth
RACE
RACE beams supply power and communications capabilities to support multiple technologies. With Crossings, components can move horizontally along the beam and away from it for maximum flexibility.
Courtesy Haworth

Haworth
Orlando
Collection of case goods and tables including single and double pedestal desks, credenzas, returns, bridges, D-top desks, corner units, vertical storage units, bookcases, lateral files, and wardrobe/storage units.
Courtesy Haworth

195

Halcon
Attache
Designed by Lauren Rottet and Richard Riveire.
"L" workstation from a collection of case pieces with work surfaces; offered in a variety of woods, finishes, and colors with optional figured veneer drawers and contrasting stained edge accents.
Desk W 60" + 24" work surface; cabinet H 86", W 144"
Courtesy Halcon

Halcon
Attache
Designed by Lauren Rottet and Richard Riveire.
Desk and credenza, offered in a variety of woods, finishes, and colors.
Desk H 29-3/4", W 72", D 36"; Credenza H 29-3/4", W 108", D 24"
Courtesy Halcon

196

Halcon
Attache
Designed by Lauren Rottet and Richard Riveire.
"U" workstation offered in a variety of woods, finishes, and colors.
H 86", W 90", D 108" (desk 36", bridge 48", work surface 24")
Courtesy Halcon

Halcon
Agenda
Designed by Brian Kenneth Graham.
"L" workstation from a collection of case pieces with work surfaces; offered in a variety of woods, finishes, and colors.
H 71", W 171", D 79" (desk 55" + work surface 24")
Courtesy Halcon

Halcon
Gemini
Designed by Edward F. Weller III.
Workwall with mobile Arc Desk and
Boby Pedestals
Workwall H 86", W 142", D 25"; Desk H
29-3/4", W 80", D 32"; Pedestals
H 21-1/2", W 15-3/4", D 20"
Courtesy Halcon

Halcon
Gemini
Mobile Kidney Desk and Boby Pedestals.
Desk H 29-3/4", W 73", D 32"
Courtesy Halcon

Halcon
Cadence
Designed by John Thiele and Brian Graham.
Desk and Credenza from collection of case pieces and work surfaces;
available in wood veneer or metallic finishes; inset wood surfaces and
curved drawer faces.
Desk H 28-3/4", W 72", D 36"; Credenza H 38-3/4", W 72", D 24"
Courtesy Halcon

Opposite page:
Halcon
Gemini
Designed by Edward F. Weller III.
Workwall, mobile Kidney Desk with distinctive geometric veneer pattern,
and Boby Pedestals.
Workwall H 86", W 110", D 25"; Desk H 29-3/4", W 73", D 32"; Pedestals
H 21-1/2", W 15-3/4", D 20"
Courtesy Halcon

Herman Miller
Display of chairs at the former
Grandville Pavilion.
Courtesy Herman Miller

Vitra
Vitramat 200 V-Programme
Office chairs with three sections -- seat with pelvic support, adjustable lumbar support, flexible backrest. Plastic shells, with or without arms.
H 34" to 38-1/2", W 19-5/8" to 23-5/8", D 17-3/4" to 22-1/2"; High Back H 40" to 45"
Photo Hans Hansen, Courtesy Vitra

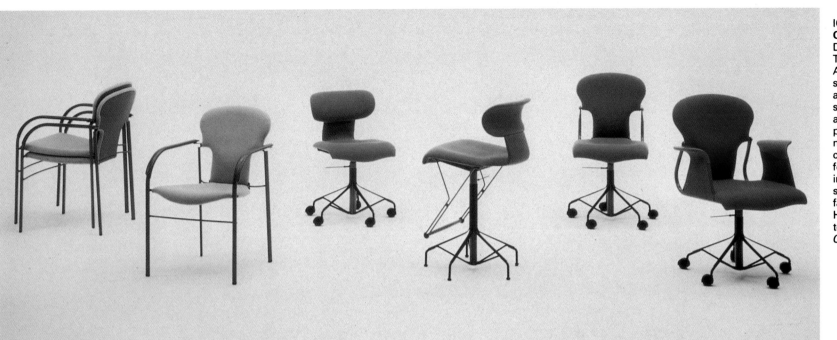

ICF
Oscar Seating
Designed by Oscar Tusquets, 1983. Adjustable office seating, Drafting Chair, and Pull-up Chair: 5-star swivel base and height adjuster (or legs on pull-up); shell of molded fiberglass covered with molded foam, upholstered inside and outside in same or contrasting fabric; leather armrests.
H 30" to 37-1/2", W 17" to 25", D 19" to 23-5/8"
Courtesy ICF

Montis (available through Luminaire)
Fantome
Designed by Marie Christine Dorner. Unupholstered shell fitted onto a high-tech base plate which is attached to the metal support; curved back offers optimum lower back support.
H 30", W 17-1/4" or 21", D 20"
Courtesy Luminaire

201

Alias (available through Luminaire)
Rolling Girl
Chair with die-cast aluminum frame, on 5-prong base with casters, changeable seat and back in natural ash or lacquered cherry wood, with fabric or leather upholstery.
H 29-1/2" to 33-1/2", W 18-1/8"
Courtesy Luminaire

DePadova (available through Luminaire)
Silver
Designed by Vico Magistretti.
Chairs with or without armrests, swivel or legs, frame of curved aluminum alloy, seat and backrest of injection-molded polypropylene.
Seat H 18-1/4" or 18" to 20-1/2", W 20" or 24".
Courtesy Luminaire

Knoll (Studio)
Pollock Executive Arm Chair
Designed by Charles Pollock, 1965.
Frame of extruded aluminum with polished chrome or black finish; outer shell integrally colored, black textured polypropylene; fabric or leather upholstered foam; tilt, swivel, and height adjustment.
H 30-5/8" to 33-1/2", W 26-1/4", D 28-1/4"
Courtesy Knoll

202

Kron
Compasso
Designed by José Luis Pérez Ortega.
Comfortable ergonomic seating collection
available in high and low back knee/tilt and
sled base models. Chairs may be specified
with single cover or with additional top
cushion upholstery.
Pictured H 36-1/2" to 41", W 23-1/2", D 21"
Courtesy Kron

Thonet
Topas Executive Swivel Chair
Designed by Erik Munnikhof, c. 1990.
Molded plywood shell construction; slim
contour profile, minimal parts, knee-tilt
mechanism for natural forward movement.
H 41-3/4", W 26-1/2", D 26-1/2"
Courtesy Thonet

Thonet
Softwear Manager Chair
Designed by Jerome Caruso, c. 1986.
With built-in flex points above lumbar
area and behind knees for optimal
comfort; wood or metal frame, fully
upholstered foam cushion seatback shell
with channel detailing.
H 34-1/2" to 39", W 24", D 26"
Courtesy Thonet

Thonet
MGT Swivel Chair
Designed by Don Petitt, c. 1981.
Oak face and maple core veneer molded
plywood frames, molded foam seats and
backs over structural thermoplastic inner
shells.
H 31-34", W 22-1/2", D 24-1/2"
Courtesy Thonet

Herman Miller
Equa 2 Chair
Designed by Bill
Stumpf and Don
Chadwick, 1995.
Work chair with
flexible one-piece
shell with H-shaped
cutout, thick foam
padding, waterfall
edges, 5-star base,
knee-tilt swivel with
lock and seat height
adjustment; adjust-
able arm kit; available
in three sizes.
H 36-1/2" to 44-1/2"
max, W 25-1/2", D 15-
3/4" to 17-3/4"
*Courtesy Herman
Miller*

Herman Miller
Equa 2 Chair
Three-quarter view.
*Courtesy Herman
Miller*

Herman Miller
Ergon 3 Chair
Designed by Bill
Stumpf, 1995.
Swivel chair with
knee-tilt with lock and
forward angle,
adjustable seat and
back height, adjust-
able arm kit, deeply
contoured seat and
back cushions and
thick foam padding;
available in four sizes.
H 35-3/4" to 45-1/4
max, W 25-1/2" to 27-
3/4", D 15-3/4" to
18-1/2"
*Courtesy Herman
Miller*

Herman Miller
Ergon 3 Chair
Designed by Bill
Stumpf, 1995.
Three high-back
Ergon 3 Management
Chairs in a team
environment.
*Courtesy Herman
Miller*

204

Herman Miller
Ergon 3 Chair
Shown with mid-back.
Courtesy Herman Miller

Herman Miller
Ergon 3 Chair
Designed by Bill Stumpf, 1995.
Five mid-back Ergon 3 Management Chairs around an Eames
Segmented Base Conference Table.
Courtesy Herman Miller

Herman Miller
Ambi Chair
Designed by Richard Holbrook, 1995.
Swivel chairs with CoActive tilt mechanism that
synchronizes the movement of chair seat and
back to reduce pressure on sitter's lumbar area;
with seat-height adjustments and options in
features and upholstery.
H 40-1/2" max, W 26-1/4", D 17"
Courtesy Herman Miller

ICF
Atlantis
Designed by Toshiyuki Kita.
Steel frame with flexible polyurethane articulating back, 5-star aluminum swivel
base, upholstered in fabric or leather.
H 34" to 37" or 35-3/4" to 38-1/2", W 26", D 26"
Courtesy ICF

Girsberger
Xerra
Designed by Dieter Stierli and the Girsberger team.
Swivel chair with dynamic synchronic mechanism, backrest and seat of molded fiberglass-reinforced
recyclable plastic, versatile appearance with wide choice of options, upholstery, and color options.
H 33" to 45", W 19" to 20-1/2", D 19-11/16"
Courtesy Girsberger

Girsberger
Consens Revival
Designed by Fritz Makiol
and the Girsberger team.
One of eight models with
one core design: normal
height or extra high
backrest, optional fixed or
adjustable armrests,
synchronous or individual
adjustment, range of easily
changed upholstery
options.
H 38-1/2" to 46", W 17-3/4"
to 24-1/2", D 16-1/2" or 17-
3/4"
Courtesy Girsberger

Girsberger
Contact
Designed by Fritz Makiol
and the Girsberger team.
Swivel chair automatically
adjusts to occupant's
weight in all positions, for
optimum contact between
chair and sitter; with
variable adjustments, and
options in sizes, features,
and upholstery.
H 42-1/2" to 49-5/8", W 25-
3/8", D 19-5/16"
Courtesy Girsberger

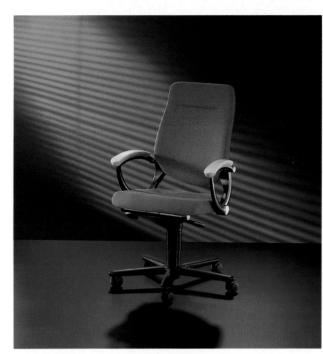

KI
Piretti 2000 Seating
Designed by Giancarlo
Piretti.
Executive and manage-
ment chairs provide
comfortable, high-value
seating; lever mechanism
enables the chair to adjust
to the weight of the
occupant; pneumatic
height adjustment,
backward seat tilt, upholstery options.
H 34-3/4" to 44-1/2", W 20-
1/2", D 17-3/4" to 19-/4"
Courtesy KI

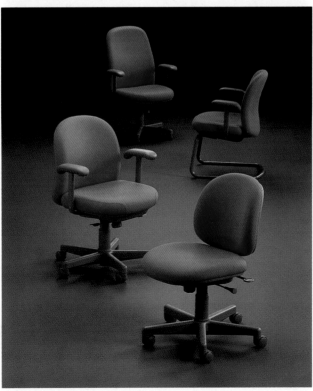

Haworth
**Improv Series High-Back
Desk Chair**
High and mid-back models
with ergonomic design:
pneumatic seat-height
adjustment, tilt tension
control, two-position back
lock, synchronized tilt
mechanism, height-
adjustable arm, molded
seat and back cushions,
waterfall seat-pan edge.
H 37-1/2", W 27-1/4", D 25"
Courtesy Haworth

207

Kron
Lauro
Designed by Jorge Pensi.
Collection of high back and low back
swivel chairs with knee tilt action and
pneumatic height adjustment, single cover
upholstery or additional sewn-in back and
seat cushions.
H 43" to 47", W 25", D seat 20"
Courtesy Kron

Metro (Steelcase Design Partnership)
Stanford
Designed by Brian Kane, c. 1988.
Executive high-back and low-back swivel
chair with upholstered seat and back and
leather-wrapped arms, molded black
polymide base on casters; options include
glides, contrasting leather or fabric arms,
contrasting color welts on seat or back.
H 35" to 38" or 45" to 48", W 26", D 28"
Courtesy Steelcase

Kron
Cavalier
Designed by Gianfranco Frattini.
Executive and conference seating
available in high, medium, and low back
heights: cast aluminum base, back and
seat frames molded plywood, cushions in
varying densities, forward tilt mechanism
incorporated into base.
H 30" to 33", 35" to 38", or 44" to 47", W
28", D 27, 28, or 29"
Courtesy Kron

Vitra
AC1 Task Chair
Designed by Antonio Citterio and Glen
Oliver Löw, c. 1988.
Armless with upholstered back shell,
pneumatic height, five-star base, adjustable
depth and tension, contrasting seat and
back.
H 34-3/4" to 39-1/2", W 19", D 19"
Courtesy Vitra

Vitra
AC Series Chairs
Designed by Antonio Citterio and Glen Oliver Löw, c. 1988.
Left to right: AC2 Executive High Back and Executive chairs on five-star base with cast aluminum frames, with variable back lock, lumbar support, and adjustable tension; AC1 High Back Task and Task Chair with flexible backrest and thickly cushioned seat; AC3 Visitor Chair on cantilever base, of tubular steel with wood arms.
Courtesy Vitra

209

Herman Miller
Eames Soft Pad Executive Chair
Designed by Charles and Ray Eames, 1969.
From the Soft Pad Collection: available in choice of
two leathers, seven fabrics; polished die-cast
aluminum five-star base, frame, and arms; tubular
steel column with enamel finish; seat height adjustment and tilt-swivel mechanism; nylon suspension;
glides or casters.
H 41" max, W 23", D 15-1/2"
Courtesy Herman Miller

Herman Miller
Eames Aluminum Group Executive Chair
Designed by Charles and Ray Eames, 1958.
Available in choice of seven fabrics; die-cast five-
star aluminum base, frame, and arms; tubular steel
column with enamel finish; layered vinyl cushioning
and nylon suspension; seat height adjustment and
tilt-swivel mechanism; casters or glides.
H 42-1/2" max, W 23", D 17"
Courtesy Herman Miller

Herman Miller
Aeron Chair
Designed by Bill Stumpf and Don Chadwick, 1994.
The lightweight and breathable Pellicle material conforms to the
sitter's body, distributes the weight evenly, and retains its original
shape. The Kinemat tilt allows the body to naturally pivot at the
ankles, knees, and hips; and the two-stage pneumatic lift provides
a wide range of height adjustment.
Three sizes: max. H 41" to 45", W 25-3/4" to 28-1/4", D 15-3/4" to
18-1/2"
Photo Nick Merrick, Hedrich-Blessing; courtesy Herman Miller.

Herman Miller
Aeron Chair
Photo Nick Merrick, Hedrich-Blessing; courtesy Herman Miller.

Haworth
TAZ Chair
Designed by 5D, 1997.
TAZ (Torsional Action Zone) provides freedom of
movement by moving backward, forward, left, and right;
excellent ergonomic support, available in three sizes,
armless or with stationary or height-adjustable arms;
choice of upholstery fabric and trim colors.
Courtesy Haworth

Haworth
TAZ Chair
Back view.
Courtesy Haworth

Haworth
TAZ Chair
Detail of back.
Courtesy Haworth

212

Top left: Girsberger
Trilax 6
Designed by Fritz
Makiol and the
Girsberger team.
Swivel chair with three-
pivot point design and
synchronous adjust-
ment system for
support and freedom
of movement, with
options such as normal
height or extra high
backrest, optional fixed
or adjustable armrests,
choice of upholstery.
H 40-1/2" to 46", W 23-
1/2", D 19"
Courtesy Girsberger

Bottom left: Girsberger
Trilax 6 Delux
Designed by Fritz
Makiol and the
Girsberger team.
Swivel chair with three-
pivot point design and
synchronic adjustment
system for support and
freedom of movement, with options such as normal height or extra high
backrest, optional fixed or adjustable armrests, choice of upholstery.
H 40-1/2" to 46", W 23-1/2", D 19"
Courtesy Girsberger

Top center: Girsberger
Pronto
Designed by Dieter Stierli and the Girsberger team.
Fixed or height-adjustable backrest, optional fixed or adjustable armrests,
synchronous or individual adjustment, range of upholstery options.
H 31-7/8" to 44", D 16-1/8" to 19-5/8"
Courtesy Girsberger

Top right: Girsberger
Pronto Drafting Stool
Designed by Dieter Stierli and the Girsberger team.
Fixed or height-adjustable backrest, synchronic or individual adjustment,
circular footrest, range of upholstery options.
H 36-1/2" to 43", W 19", D 19-1/4"
Courtesy Girsberger

Bottom right: Girsberger
Consens Drafting Stool
Designed by Fritz Makiol and the Girsberger team.
Available in two seat widths, individual adjustment mechanism, optional fixed
or adjustable armrests, easily replaceable seat and back cushions, circular
footrest.
H 35-1/4" to 48-3/4", W 17-3/4", D 17-1/2" or 18"
Courtesy Girsberger

Top left: KI
Perry Chair
Designed by Charles Perry.
High-density stacking chair with passive ergonomic support, has articulating backrest; steel frame with polypropylene seat and back; available in armless, armchair, and tablet arm models.
H 32-1/2", W 19-3/4" or 23-3/8", D 21-1/2"
Courtesy KI

Top center: KI
Perry Chair
Articulating backrest.
Courtesy KI

Bottom left: KI
Piretti Xylon Chair
Designed by Giancarlo Piretti.
Articulating back, spring action backrest; wood or metal frames; beech plywood seat and back in natural or stained finish.
H 32-1/4", W 16-7/8" to 23-1/2", D 20-7/8"
Courtesy KI

Haworth
Kinetics Tempo Series
Lounge seating with modular, preconfigured, or freestanding components with adjustable foot glides, curved "floating" chair arms; shown preconfigured with table.
H 33-3/4", W 67-5/8 three seats, 68" two seats & table, D 25-1/2"
Courtesy Haworth

Haworth
Kinetics Tempo Series
Lounge seating with modular, preconfigured, or freestanding components with adjustable foot glides, curved "floating" chair arms; shown fully upholstered in leather, with elastic webbing suspension.
H 33-3/4", W 30-1/4 and 52-1/4", D 29-1/2"
Courtesy Haworth

Haworth
Improv Series Guest Chair
Stacking capacity; wide range of upholstery options; optional ganging connector, tables, or tablet arms.
H 32", W 22", D 21-1/2"
Courtesy Haworth

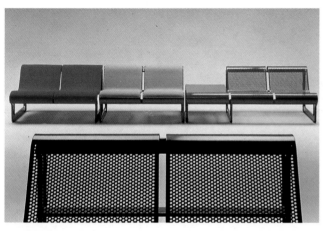

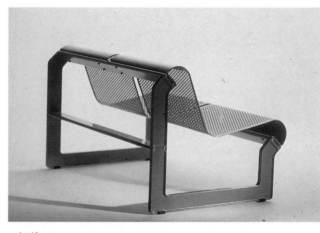

Artifort
Lagos
Designed by Nel Verschuuren.
Seating unit for public areas in 1, 2, 3, or 4-seat sizes, with
seat sections of perforated steel plate on an aluminum base
(right); with optional upholstery on a pre-formed shell fixed to
the steel seat (left).
H 28", W 22-1/2" to 93-1/4", D 31-1/2"
Courtesy Artifort

Artifort
Lagos
Designed by Nel Verschuuren.
Two-seat unupholstered unit.
H 28", W 46", D 31-1/2"
Courtesy Artifort

Vitra
Area
Designed by Antonio Citterio and Oliver Löw.
Two or three-seat sofa with individual backrests;
frame of cast aluminum with chrome finish; seat
upholstered foam on wood frame.
Courtesy Vitra

Opposite page:
Left: Artifort
Domino
Designed by Wolfgang Müller Deisig.
Multifunctional stackable and linking chair; seat and back of pressed and stained or
lacquered beechwood, with or without upholstery, arms coated or polished aluminum.
H 32-5/8", W 19-5/8" or 22-1/2", D 21-1/4"
Courtesy Artifort

Right: Thonet
Linx Modular Seating
Designed by Thonet Design Staff, c. 1989.
Modular seating of tubular steel frame and only four basic components connected by
exposed linking device; table with laminated top.
Seat H 29-3/4", W 25", D 31"; table H 13-3/4", W 25" or 48", D 31"
Courtesy Thonet

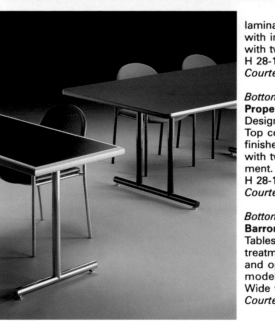

Top left: Knoll (Studio)
Propeller Training Tables
Designed by Emanuela Frattini, 1994.
H 28-1/2", W 60/30" or 72/36", D 26" or 31"
Courtesy Knoll

Top right: Knoll (Studio)
Propeller Training Table
Designed by Emanuela Frattini, 1994.
Portable table of trapezoid shape for versatile configurations; top of 1-1/4" 5-ply hollow-core construction, covered in plastic laminate; molded seamless urethane edge with integral color; legs of extruded aluminum with two channels for wire mangement.
H 28-1/2", W 60/30" or 72/36", D 26" or 31"
Courtesy Knoll

Bottom left: Knoll (Studio)
Propeller Conference Table
Designed by Emanuela Frattini, 1994.
Top covered in laminate or wood veneer, finished edges, 0-2 grommets, S-shaped leg with two separate channels for wire management.
H 28-1/2", W 60" to 96", D 42" to 60"
Courtesy Knoll

Bottom right: KI
Barron Tables
Tables with T or TT-base and five edge treatments in 15 colors; with wire channels and optional spacing bumper with folding models.
Wide variety of sizes.
Courtesy KI

7: Accessories

Top right: Haworth
Crossings Computer/CAD Stand
For intensive computer applications,
with feet or casters; cutaway is 15"
deep by 24-1/2" wide.
H 26" to 30", W 56", D 32"
Courtesy Haworth

Bottom right: Haworth
Crossings Computer Cart
Mobile surface for personal computer,
keyboard, and mouse; with feet or
casters.
H 39", W 26", D 36-1/2"
Courtesy Haworth

Herman Miller
Scooter
Designed by Jack Kelley, 1986.
Versatile keyboard stand with aluminum
base and support column, with height
adjustment and tilt mechanism with range
of 20 degrees, optional foam hand rest.
H 22" to 30", tray W 22", D 11" or 11-3/4"
Courtesy Herman Miller

Herman Miller
Scooter
In office setting.
Courtesy Herman Miller

Knoll (Studio)
Propeller Cart
Designed by Emanuela Frattini, 1994.
Aluminum legs on casters, lower shelf; in
two sizes.
H 27" or 28-1/2", W 36" or 44", D 20" or
24"
Courtesy Knoll

Thonet
Vienna Café Costumer
Designed by Michael Thonet's sons, c.
1860.
By 1887 costumers, hat racks, and music
stands were a few of the utilitarian objects
made of the fluid steambent wood; walnut
finish.
H 74", W 25"
Courtesy Thonet

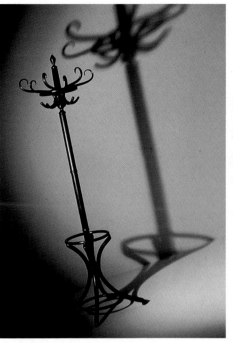

Vitra
Wardrobe/Coatstand
Designed by Borek Sipek, 1989/91.
Three leg metal frame, lacquered
hammerite; two turned wood ellipses;
brass tube; steel tube with red lacquered
finish; halogen light.
H 78-3/4", W 23-3/4", D 23-3/4".
Courtesy Vitra

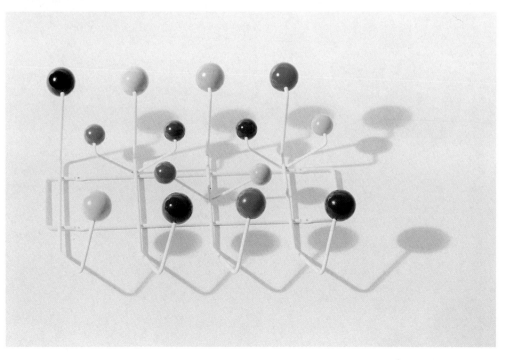

Herman Miller
Eames Hang-It-All
Designed by Charles and Ray Eames,
1953.
Steel rod frame with white powder coat;
painted solid maple balls in nine colors.
H 14-5/8", W 19-3/4", D 6-1/2"
Courtesy Herman Miller

Top left: Brueton Industries
Reflections III
Designed by J. Wade Beam, 1990.
Mirror in various sizes and shapes -- round, square, or rectangular.
Courtesy Brueton

Top center left: Brueton Industries
Fist Mirror/Console
Designed by Stanley Jay Friedman, 1992.
Circular mirror gripping attached light fixture on each side, of
stainless steel in choice of finishes; console top in acid wash
stainless steel, stone, or wood.
Mirror DM 42" or 48", suggested total H 69"
Courtesy Brueton

Top center right: Brueton Industries
Alpha Mirror
Designed by Stanley Jay Friedman, 1991.
Rectangular mirror in acid wash gray, various sizes such as 24" x
36" or 30" x 48"
Courtesy Brueton

Top right: Brueton Industries
Reflections II
Designed by J. Wade Beam, 1990.
Square 48" or 60"; or rectangular 36" x 48", 36" x 60", or 48" x 60"
Courtesy Brueton

Bottom left: Brueton Industries
Crown Mirror & Console
Designed by Stanley Jay Friedman, 1992.
Rectangular mirror with architectural base and detached over-
hang.
H 76-1/2", W 34", D 16-1/2"
Courtesy Brueton

Herman Miller
Molded Plywood Folding Screen
Designed by Charles and Ray Eames, 1946.
Light ash face veneer with maple inner plies; woven polypropylene mesh connects plywood sections.
H 68", W 60", D 2-1/4"
Courtesy Herman Miller

Baleri Italia (available through Luminaire)
Cartoons
Designed by Luigi Baroli, c. 1992.
Screen with self-bearing structure stiffened with die-cast aluminum, body of recyclable corrugated paperboard.
H 70", L 15" to 157"
Courtesy Luminaire

Vitra
Paper Basket/Umbrella Stand
Designed by Borek Sipek, 1989.
Sheet metal with matte silver lacquer, brass tops.
H 21-3/4", W 15-3/4", D 15-3/4"
Courtesy Vitra

Tecta
Bauhaus-Cradle
Designed by Peter Keler, 1922.
Cradle with two steel pipe end rings supporting a lacquered container shaped like an inverted gable roof, based on Wassily Kandinsky's investigation of the synthetic relationship between color and form.
DM 35-3/4", L 38-1/2"
Courtesy Tecta

Further Reading

Abercrombie, Stanley. *George Nelson: the Design of Modern Design*. Cambridge: MIT Press, 1995.

Amery, Colin. *Pioneers of Modern Furniture*. London: Fischer Fine Art, 1991.

Baroni, Daniele. *The Furniture of Gerrit Thomas Rietveld*. Woodbury: Barron's, 1980.

Benton, Tim & B. Campbell-Cole, eds. *Tubular Steel Furniture*. London: Art Book Co., 1979.

Billcliffe, Roger. *Charles Rennie Mackintosh: The Complete Furniture, Furniture Drawings and Interior Designs*. 3rd ed. New York: E.P. Dutton, 1986.

Caplan, Ralph. *The Design of Herman Miller*. New York: Whitney Library of Design, 1976.

Conway, Hazel. *Ernest Race*. London: Design Council, 1982.

Detroit Institute of Arts. *Design in America: The Cranbrook Vision 1925-1950*. New York: Harry N. Abrams, 1983.

Dormer, Peter. *Design Since 1945*. London: Thames and Hudson, 1993.

Droste, Magdalena, et al. *Marcel Breuer Design*. Köln: Taschen, 1992.

Edwards, Clive D. *Twentieth-Century Furniture: Materials, Manufacture and Markets*. Manchester and New York: Manchester University Press, 1994.

Eidelberg, Martin, ed. *Design 1935-1965: What Modern Was*. New York: Harry N. Abrams, 1991.

Emery, Marc. *Furniture by Architects*. New York: Harry N. Abrams, 1983; expanded edition 1988.

Fahr-Becker, Gabriele. *Wiener Werkstaette 1903-1932*. Köln: Taschen, 1995.

Fehrman, Cherie and Kenneth Fehrman. *Postwar Interior Design 1945-1960*. New York: Van Nostrand Reinhold, 1987.

Fiell, Charlotte & Peter. *Modern Furniture Classics Since 1945*. Washington D.C.: AIA Press, 1991.

-------. *Modern Chairs*. Köln, Germany: Taschen, 1993.

Filippo, Alison. *Charles Rennie Mackintosh as a Designer of Chairs*. Milan: documenti di Casabella, 1973.

Gandy, Charles D. and Susan Zimmermann-Stedham. *Contemporary Classics: Furniture of the Masters*. New York: Whitney Library of Design, 1990 (originally McGraw-Hill, 1981).

Garner, Philippe. *Twentieth-Century Furniture*. New York: Van Nostrand Reinhold, 1980.

-------. *Sixties Design*. Köln: Taschen, 1996.

-------. *Eileen Gray: Designer and Architect*. Köln: Taschen Benedikt Verlag, 1993.

Glaeser, Ludwig. *Ludwig Mies van der Rohe: Furniture and Furniture Drawings*. New York: Museum of Modern Art, 1977.

Greenberg, Cara. *Mid-Century Modern: Furniture of the 1950s*. New York: Harmony, 1984; reprinted 1995.

Habegger, Jerryll and Joseph H. Osman. *Sourcebook of Modern Furniture. 2nd edition*. New York: W. W. Norton, 1997, 1989.

Hanks, David A. *Innovative Furniture in America from 1800 to the Present*. New York: Horizon Press, 1981.

Heinz, Thomas A. *Frank Lloyd Wright Furniture Portfolio*. Layton, Utah: Gibbs Smith, 1993.

Hiesinger, Kathryn B. & George H. Marcus. *Landmarks of Twentieth-Century Design: An Illustrated Handbook*. New York: Abbeville, 1993.

Hennessey, William J. *Modern Furnishings for the Home. Volumes 1 & 2*. New York: Reinhold, 1952 & 1956.

Herman Miller Furniture Co. *The Herman Miller Collection: 1952 Catalog*. Reprinted, New York: Acanthus, 1995.

-------. *The Herman Miller Collection: 1955/56 Catalog*. Reprinted, Atglen, Pennsylvania: Schiffer, 1997.

Horn, Richard. *Fifties Style*. New York: Friedman/Fairfax, 1993.

Hunter, Sam. *Isamu Noguchi*. New York: Abbeville, 1978.

Jackson, Lesley. *The New Look: Design in the Fifties*. New York: Thames Hudson, 1991.

-------. *Contemporary Architecture and Interiors of the 1950s*. London: Phaidon, 1994.

Jaffé, Hans Ludwig C. *De Stijl 1917-1931*. Cambridge: Harvard U. Press, 1986.

Kardon, Janet, ed. *Craft in the Machine Age 1920-1945*. New York: Harry N. Abrams and American Craft Museum, 1995.

King, Carol Soucek. *Furniture: Architects' and Designers' Originals*. Glen Cove, New York: PBC International, 1994.

Kirkham, Pat. *Charles and Ray Eames: Designers of the Twentieth Century*. Cambridge: MIT, 1995.

Knobel, Lance. *Office Furniture: Twentieth-Century Design*. New York: E.P. Dutton, 1987.

Knoll Group. *75 Years of Bauhaus Design 1919-1994*. New York: Knoll Group, 1994.

Larrabee, Eric & Massimo Vignelli. *Knoll Design*. New York: Harry N. Abrams, 1981.

Lind, Carla. *The Wright Style*. New York: Simon & Schuster, 1992.

Lipman, Jonathan. *Frank Lloyd Wright and the Johnson Wax Buildings*. New York: Rizzoli, 1986.

Mang, Karl. *History of Modern Furniture*. New York: Harry N. Abrams, 1978.

McFadden, David Revere. *Scandinavian Modern Design 1880-1980*. New York: Harry N. Abrams, 1982.

Meadmore, Clement. *The Modern Chair: Classics in Production*. New York: Van Nostrand Reinhold, 1975.

Nelson, George. *Chairs*. New York: Whitney, 1953; reprinted New York: Acanthus, 1994.

-------. *Display*. New York: Whitney, 1953.

-------. *Storage*. New York: Whitney, 1954.

Neuhart, John, Marilyn Neuhart, & Ray Eames. *Eames Design*. New York: Harry N. Abrams, 1991.

Noyes, Eliot N. *Organic Design in Home Furnishings*. Catalog. New York: Museum of Modern Art, 1941.

Ostergard, Derek E. *Bent Wood and Metal Furniture 1850-1946*. New York: American Federation of Arts, 1987.

Pearce, Christopher. *Fifties Source Book: A Visual Guide to the Style of a Decade*. Secaucus, New Jersey: Chartwell, 1990.

Piña, Leslie. *Fifties Furniture*. Atglen, Pennsylvania: Schiffer, 1996.

-------. *Classic Herman Miller*. Atglen, Pennsylvania: Schiffer, 1998.

-------. *Herman Miller Interior Views*. Atglen, Pennsylvania: Schiffer, 1998.

Pulos, Arthur J. *American Design Ethic: A History of Industrial Design to 1940*. Cambridge: MIT Press, 1983.

-------. *The American Design Adventure 1940-1975*. Cambridge: MIT Press, 1988.

Radice, Barbara. *Memphis; Research, Experiences, Results, Failures, and Successes of New Design*. New York: Thames and Hudson, 1995.

Rieman, Timothy D. and Jean M. Burks. *The Complete Book of Shaker Furniture*. New York: Harry N. Abrams, 1993.

Robsjohn-Gibbings, T.H. *Good-Bye Mr. Chippendale*. New York: Alfred J. Knopf, 1945.

Saarinen, Eero and Aline B. Saarinen. *Eero Saarinen on His Work*. New Haven: Yale University Press, 1962.

Santini, Pier Carlo. *The Years of Italian Design: A Portrait of Cesare Cassina*. Milan: Electa, 1981.

Schildt, Göran. *Alvar Aalto: the Decisive Years*. New York: Rizzoli, 1986.

Schweiger, Werner J. *Wiener Werkstaette: Design in Vienna 1903-*

1932. New York: Abbeville, 1984.

Sembach, Klaus-Jürgen, et al. *Twentieth-Century Furniture Design*. Köln: Taschen, 1989.

Sharp, Dennis et al, eds. *Pel and Tubular Steel Furniture of the Thirties*. London: Architectural Associations, 1977.

Smithsonian Institution. *A Modern Consciousness: J.D. DePree, Florence Knoll*. Exhibition catalog. Washington D.C.: Smithsonian Institution Press, 1975.

Sparke, Penny. Furniture: *Twentieth-Century Design*. New York: E.P. Dutton, 1986.

-------. *Italian Design 1870 to the Present*. London: Thames and Hudson, 1988.

Steelcase, Inc. *Steelcase: The First 75 Years*. Grand Rapids: Steelcase, Inc. 1987.

Stimpson, Miriam. *Modern Furniture Classics*. New York: Whitney Library of Design, 1987.

Thonet Industries. *Thonet Bentwood & Other Furniture: the 1904 Illustrated Catalog*. Reprint. New York: Dover, 1980.

Tøjner, Poul Erik and Kjeld Vindam. *Arne Jacobsen: Architect and Designer*. København: Dansk Design Center, 1994.

von Vegesack, Alexander. *Thonet: Classical Furniture in Bent Wood and Tubular Steel*. New York, 1997.

von Vegesack, Alexander et al. eds. *100 Masterpieces from the Vitra Design Museum Collection*. Weil am Rhein: Vitra Design Museum, 1996.

Whitney Museum of Art. *High Styles: Twentieth-Century American Design*. New York: Whitney Museum, 1985.

Wilk, Christopher. *Marcel Breuer: Furniture and Interiors*. New York: Museum of Modern Art, 1981.

-------. *Thonet: 150 Years of Furniture*. Woodbury, New York: Barrons, 1980.

Zahle, Erik, ed. *A Treasury of Scandinavian Design*. New York: Golden Press, 1961.

Zelleke, Ghenete et al. *Against the Grain: Bentwood Furniture from the Collection of Fern and Manfred Steinfeld*. Chicago: Art Institute of Chicago, 1993.

Sources: Manufacturers & Suppliers

Acerbis International
Via Brusaporto 31
I-24068 Seriate
Bergamo, Italy
(available through Luminaire)

Alias
Via Leonardo da Vinci 29
24064 Grumello Del Monte
Bergamo, Italy
(available through ICF and Luminaire)

Alivar
Via Pisana 45
50021 Barberino val d'Elsa-Firenze
Italy
(available through Palazzetti)

Arc Age
15751 Stagg Street
Van Nuys CA 91406
818.786.2288

Artifort
St. Annalaan 23
6214 AA Maastricht
Netherlands

Baker Furniture
1661 Monroe NW
Grand Rapids MI 49505-4658
616.361.7321
800.592.2537

Baleri Italia
Via Trento 10
24100 Curno
Bergamo, Italy
(available through Luminaire)

B&B Italia
150 E. 58th Street
New York NY 10155
800.872.1697
(available through Luminaire)

Brayton (see Steelcase)
Brayton International Inc.
255 Swathmore Avenue
High Point NC 27263
800.627.6770
910.434.4151

Breuton Industries
145-68 228th Street
Springfield Gardens, NY 11413
718.527.3000

Cappellini
Via Marconi 35
22060 Arosio
Como, Italy
(Available through Luminaire)

Casigliani
Via P. Barsanti, 4
56014 Ospedaletto
Pisa, Italy
050.981091
(available through Luminaire)

Cassina USA Inc
200 McKay Road
Huntington Station NY 11746
800.770.3568
516.423.4560

ClassiCon
Perchtingerstrasse 8
D-81379 Munich, Germany
(available through Luminaire)

DePadova s.r.l.
Corso Venezia 14
20121 Milano, Italy
02.76008413
(available through Luminaire)

Design America
4200 Aurora Street
Coral Gables FL 33146
800.367.3003

Driade
Via Padana Inferiore 12/A
I-29012 Fossadello di Caorso
Piacenza, Italy
(available through Luminaire)

Girsberger office seating companies
with headquarters in Bützberg, Switzerland.
Girsberger Industries
Box 1476
Smithfield NC 27577
919.934.0545
http://www.smith-hawken.com

Halcon
1811 Second Avenue NW
Stewartville MN 55976
507.533.4235

Halifax
(available through Luminaire)

Haworth, Inc.
One Haworth Center
Holland MI 49423-9576
800.344.2600 ext. 45
616.393.3000
www.haworth-furn.com

Herman Miller, Inc., is an international
company. For the location of the showroom, sales office, or dealer nearest you,
call 800.851.1196.
Herman Miller for the Home, call
800.646.4400

ICF, Inc. (International Contract Furnishings)
10 Maple Street
Norwood NJ 07648
800.237.1625
201.784.0200

Interlübke
Postfach 1660
D-4840 Rheda-Wiedenbrueck
Germany
(available through Luminaire)

Kartell
Via Delle Industrie 1
I-20082 Noviglio
Milano, Italy
(available through Luminaire)

KI (Krueger International)
1330 Bellevue St.
Green Bay WI 54302
800.424.2432

Knoll
105 Wooster Street
New York NY 10012
212.343.4000
800.445.5045

Kron USA
1631 S. Dixie Highway
Pompano Beach FL 33060
954.941.0800

Luminaire
301 West Superior
Chicago IL 60610
312.664.9582

Memphis s.r.l.
Via Olivetti 9
20010 Pregnana
Milan, Italy
02.93290663

Metro (see Steelcase)
Metropolitan Furniture Corporation
1635 Rollins Road
Burlingame CA 94010-2301
415.697.7900
www.metrofurniture.com

Montis
Postbus 153
Steenstraat 2
5100 AD Dongen, Netherlands
(available through Luminaire)

Palazzetti Inc.
515 Madison Avenue
New York NY 10022
212.832.1199

Shaker Workshops
14 S. Pleasant Street
Ashburnham MA 01430-8001
508.827.9900
shaker@shakerworkshops.com

Smith & Hawken
117 East Strawberry Drive
Mill Valley CA 94941
415.389.8300
www.smith-hawkin.com

Steelcase
Grand Rapids MI 49501-1967
For general information about
Steelcase products
contact your local dealership:
800.333.9939
or visit the web site at
www.steelcase.com

Steelcase Design Partnership
Box 1967
901 44th Street SE
Grand Rapids MI 49510-1967
616.475.2000

Tecno
Via Bigli 22
I-20121 Milano, Italy
(available through Luminaire)

Tecta Möbel
D-37697 Lauenförde
Germany
0.52.73.37890

Tendo Co, Ltd.
810 Midarekawa
Tendo Yamagata 994
Japan
0236.53.3121

Thonet International
403 Meacham Road
Statesville NC 28677
704.878.2222

Vecta (see Steelcase)
Box 534013
1800 South Great Southwest Parkway
Grand Prairie TX 75051
972.641.2860

Vitra GmbH
Charles-Eames-Strasse 2
D-79576 Weil am Rhein
Germany

Vitra, Inc.
149 Fifth Avenue
New York NY 10010
212.539.1900

Wogg
Im Hos 10
Ch-5405
Baden-Dattwil, Switzerland
(available through Luminaire)

Zero U.S. Corp.
85 Industrial Circle
Lincoln RI 02865
401.724.4470

Zero Showroom
560 Broadway
New York NY 10012
212.925.3615

Designer Index

Sources Index